HAPPY VEGAN CHRISTMAS

HAPPY VEGAN CHRISTMAS

Karoline Jönsson

PAVILION

FIRST PUBLISHED IN THE UNITED KINGDOM IN 2019 BY
PAVILION
43 GREAT ORMOND STREET
LONDON
WC1N 3HZ

COPYRIGHT © PAVILION BOOKS COMPANY LTD 2019

ORIGINAL TITLE: DEN GODA GRÖNA JULEN
TEXT AND PHOTOGRAPHY © KAROLINE JÖNSSON AND NORSTEDTS, STOCKHOLM
FIRST PUBLISHED BY NORSTEDTS, SWEDEN, IN 2017.
PUBLISHED BY AGREEMENT WITH NORSTEDTS AGENCY.

ISBN 978-1-91162-458-5

A CIP CATALOGUE RECORD FOR THIS BOOK IS AVAILABLE FROM THE BRITISH
LIBRARY.

10 9 8 7 6 5 4 3 2 1

REPRODUCTION BY JK MORRIS AB, VÄRNAMO
PRINTED AND BOUND BY 1010 PRINTING INTERNATIONAL LTD, CHINA
WWW.PAVILIONBOOKS.COM

I OFTEN CLAIM TO BE A FAN of every season of the year – that each month has its own charm. Yet, I have to say when the warmer part of autumn has come to an end, when the leaves have fallen off the trees and the icy, biting wind blows straight through the thickest coat, and the weather is grey for three weeks straight, Christmas appears on the horizon like a guardian angel. For me, the festive season is warmth in the cold, the light in the darkness and the magical time when everything turns, since once Christmas is over the winter solstice has come and gone; the light has turned and is returning again.

Here, far up in the north, the seasons really make their mark. Traditionally, we have had to make use of all the resources that we've been able to muster to fulfil our need for vitamins and minerals during the winter months. In the past, when the stockpiles had been emptied and the winter food started to dry up by the start of spring, both humans and animals would have had to resort to drinking birch sap and chewing on spruce shoots. People relied on growing and preserving their own food, from baking long-lasting bark bread and drying herbs to using salt, sugar, smoke and acid to ensure foods lasted longer. It was important to grow everything, including crops for harvesting in early summer; cabbages that could be left in the ground until winter; and fruit and vegetables that can be stored for a long time, such as pumpkins, apples, onions and beetroots.

Nowadays, even though we're no longer dependent on the early vegetable season and building up stores to last until the following spring, I get a lot of satisfaction from my hobby, gardening, and being able to harvest, gather, preserve, store and fill up my own supplies. This enables me to serve the crops from the summer and harvest season during the year's leaner months.

Many of the recipes in this book are based on what I like to grow and store in various ways throughout the year, or things that can still be harvested in December in Sweden. In the book

I share tips on how I prepare for a lavish Christmas celebration as well as the barren winter months by making the most of the apple harvest, freezing wild berries and drying mushrooms. It's time to celebrate the earth's good produce in the kitchen, and this book is, of course, all about how to create a gloriously vegan festive spread.

Christmas is the time of year for sharing and when we're at our most generous; we open our hearts and put a few extra coins in charity collection boxes, we buy each other gifts and gather together family and friends. Imagine if we could show the same genuine love towards all animals, whether they have paws, hooves, fins or wings.

In this book, the recipes are all kind to animals, the environment and yourself. They are all made from plant-based ingredients and that's how I like to eat all the time, due to the simple fact that I don't need meat to survive and to get all the nutrients and protein that my body requires for good health. I believe that many of us who choose a vegan diet do it simply because we don't want to eat animals – not because we don't like the flavour of meat. This has led me to look at our traditional Swedish dishes, cakes and drinks and adapt them so they're all completely plant based. That said, many of the recipes are entirely new and without the ambition to mimic meat dishes. My hope is that this book will give everyone enough 'fruit flesh on the bones' to cook up a magical vegan shimmering Christmas.

I wish everyone a truly merry Christmas, not just fellow human beings, but all animals too.

KAROLINE JÖNSSON

WINTER FOOD

THROUGHOUT THE YEAR, I notice very clearly how my body has different needs when it comes to food. In spring, I crave fresh foods, salads, chlorophyll-packed leaves and shoots, and sprightly flavours such as coriander (cilantro), ginger and citrus. During the summer months I find it difficult to enjoy warm food, especially during the day, and prefer simple meals using fresh ingredients, and more fruit and sweet ingredients.

In the autumn and winter, when the body to a certain extent follows nature into a state of hibernation and calm, all I want is comfort food; it should be rich, warm, nutritious and filling. The body is tired, cold and doesn't get any extra energy from the weather and the fleeting daylight. At this time of year I crave soups, stews, rich spice blends and traditional comfort food. It's perhaps no coincidence that the ingredients traditionally used during this time are the ones that are rich and filling, and come into their own when cooked in the right way.

For those who want to continue to eat a lot of raw food during the winter months, you can with a little help from spices to achieve a warming, rich flavour. Chilli, cinnamon, ginger and cardamom are examples of spices that will warm you

from the inside out. For instance, a raw, smooth vegetable soup has a warming effect if it's flavoured with chilli. You can also achieve the rich umami flavours found in a lot of cooked food by using tamari, sun-dried tomatoes, dried mushrooms, tahini or nut butters.

On the whole, I like to follow the seasons and eat things that are available right here and right now. That's why a lot of the basic ingredients in the recipes in this book are mainly in season in the winter months. However, if there's a time of year when I think buying imported fruits can be justified then this is it as we have very little homegrown fruit during the winter in Sweden. Buying mangoes or melons in the middle of summer or at harvest time, when we have loads of homegrown garden berries, plums, apples, cherries and pears, is in my opinion less climate smart than eating citrus fruits, persimmons or pomegranates in the leaner winter months.

It's a good idea to make the most of the freezer during the winter. The abundance of fruit and berries or summer vegetables that were in season a few months earlier can still be seasonal if frozen (or preserved) in time, whether they be homegrown courgettes (zucchini) or foraged blackberries, or even frozen shop-bought spinach from the supermarket.

MY PANTRY

FRESH FOODS

In the larder I have apples, onions and winter squash of different kinds, colours and shapes. I store garlic at room temperature. In the vegetable patch you'll still find kale and cavolo nero, beetroot (beets) and Jerusalem artichokes.

FROZEN FOODS

The freezer is full of things that don't keep for long when fresh, such as courgettes (zucchini), green beans, field mushrooms, birch sap, apple juice, blackberries, sea buckthorn, raspberries, aronia berries and other summer berries.

PRESERVES, JAMS AND CORDIALS

In my fridge you'll find rows of jars full of strawberry compote, green tomato marmalade, spruce shoot syrup, pickled cucumber, lingonberry jam and pickled beetroots (beets).

DRIED FOODS

I keep summer's lovely herbs, leaves, berries, fruits and flowers dried in glass jars. Whole dried rosehips can be boiled then blended, strained and sweetened to be served as a homemade rosehip drink. You'll also find dried apple and pear slices.

FRESH SEASONAL INGREDIENTS

red, yellow, white and Chioggia beetroot (beets), potato, carrot, parsnip, salsify, parsley root, celeriac (celery root), daikon, Jerusalem artichoke

pumpkin, red kuri squash, butternut squash, spaghetti squash

brown onion, red onion, shallot, garlic, leek, pearl onion, white onion

swede (rutabaga), kale, cavolo nero, Brussels sprouts, white cabbage, red cabbage, Savoy cabbage, cauliflower, kohlrabi, Chinese leaf cabbage

sprouts, shoots, cress, chicory (endive), sage, parsley

oyster mushroom, truffles

apple, sloe berries, juniper berries

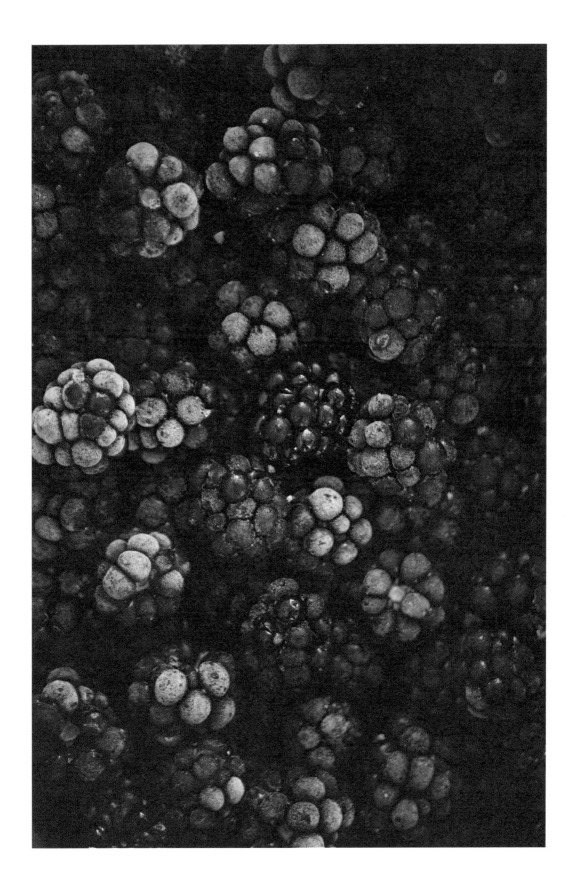

STOCKING UP THE LARDER

Vegan cooking may require a bit of a rethink of the kitchen for some. Even though it's possible to make plant-based versions of old traditional favourites, there may be gaps to fill with new ingredients. If you remove meat, fish, dairy and eggs from your diet you will, of course, have to consider adding alternative ingredients. Here, I've listed some basic ingredients that I always have at home, and which help me to organize everyday meals, parties and even Christmas feasts fairly simply and easily.

LENTILS

Puy lentils are small in size and have a beautiful mottled grey-green colour. They keep their texture when cooked and are therefore especially suited to robust salads. Black beluga lentils have the same properties. Red lentils, on the other hand, can become mushy and have a much shorter cooking time – around 10 minutes – which makes them fantastic in dishes where you don't want them to keep their shape, such as in soups or lentil bolognese, for example. I use green lentils more rarely; they don't become mushy as easily as the red ones, but neither do they keep their firm texture as well as Puy or beluga lentils, and they therefore have never been a favourite of mine.

BEANS AND PEAS

I'm a bean lover and see legumes as the most natural of my protein sources. I like to use a range of different beans, everything from

dried to frozen and canned, and in various shapes, sizes and colours. All beans have slightly different characteristics and ways to use them, but can usually be swapped for other varieties in the legume family if you don't want to fill your shelves with too many types.

Mung beans are perfect for sprouting, while large and small white beans are great for blending into different kinds of spreads or dips, for using in pasta sauces, as a topping for a bowl of smooth soup or for thickening soups and stews – just blend into a purée and stir in. More colourful varieties such as kidney beans and black beans are nice to use in stews and chillies. Chickpeas (garbanzos) I use for hummus, but they are also wonderful coated in a blend of spices and toasted, then served sprinkled over salads. Yellow peas, which are grown in Sweden, can often be used instead of chickpeas if you're looking for a more typical Scandinavian dish.

It's great to have green peas and edamame (soya) beans in the freezer, and they only need boiling for a couple of minutes before they are ready to eat. The peas can be blended into soup or hummus in no time at all.

QUINOA

Quinoa is a great plant source of protein, just like legumes, with a lot of different uses. I use quinoa as a base for everything from patties to pastry cases, in salads, stews and porridge and as an alternative to rice.

NUTS

Within plant-based dishes, nuts are often used a bit more creatively than in meat-based ones. Almonds and hazelnuts can be turned into the most fantastic nut milks and also into cheese and yogurt. Also, cashew nuts are especially suitable for making into cheese, yogurt, cream cheese, frostings, custard, mayonnaise, soured cream and cheesecake. Cashews give drinks such as milkshakes a thick and creamy consistency. Simply put, they are a great all-round nut.

SEEDS

Just like nuts, seeds are a great source of good fats and protein. Sunflower seeds, unhulled white and black sesame seeds, pumpkin seeds, hulled hemp seeds, linseeds and chia seeds are the ones I always have at home. I use sunflower seeds the most – see my vegan 'meatballs' on page 107 – since their natural flavour goes well with many other foods.

Flours made from chia seeds and psyllium husk are a perfect alternative to eggs when baking and you need something extra to bind the dough. This is because linseeds, chia seeds and psyllium husk turn into a gel-like mixture when soaked. The gel has binding properties and can be used in such dishes as raw food puddings and seed crackers.

SUPERFOODS

Superfoods have in my opinion been unfairly mocked and misunderstood. This is because many believe that superfoods are just 'trendy' ingredients that come from far away and refers to ingredients like chia seeds, goji berries and maca powder. Yet the word 'super' is simply used to highlight ingredients that are especially nutritious. Examples of Swedish superfoods that I keep in my cupboard are dried blueberries, sea buckthorn, aronia berries, cranberries, nettles and rosehips, as well as powders made from freeze-dried lingonberries, blueberries and cranberries. Other seasonal 'super' ingredients are beetroot (beets) and kale – so the food doesn't have to come from far away to qualify as a superfood.

In addition, I like to stock up on hulled hemp seeds, cacao nibs, coconut flakes, matcha powder and spirulina to use as toppings for porridge, smoothie bowls and blended banana ice cream.

SWEETENERS

Coconut sugar is an unrefined sugar with a nice caramel flavour that behaves in a similar way to granulated sugar, but is perceived as being less sweet.

Dates are wonderful to use as a sweetener in raw food 'baking'. They are nature's own caramel that can be blended into a caramel sauces, ice creams, shakes and similar. Date syrup is dark in colour and has a distinctive flavour. It can be found in Middle Eastern food stores and health food shops.

Agave syrup is golden in colour and an efficient sweetener without adding too much flavour.

Maple syrup has a bit more flavour than agave, but is still fairly neutral in comparison to date syrup.

GRAINS AND FLOURS

Spelt flour has become my go-to flour for baking bread, in place of standard wheat flour. It's an older wheat variety that behaves similarly to standard wheat flour, so any recipes listing spelt flour can be replaced with plain (all-purpose) flour, if you prefer.

Cornmeal is gluten free and has a lovely golden yellow colour. I use it for cornbread and tortillas or as a binding agent in corn or vegetable burgers.

Gram (chickpea) flour is rich in protein and gluten free, perfect for using in vegetable burgers.

Buckwheat flour has, in my opinion, a fairly prominent buckwheat flavour, which, funnily enough, whole hulled buckwheat hasn't once soaked and rinsed. I found the flavour very difficult to get used to when I first tried it a few years ago, but it has since started to grow on me. For me, buckwheat flour is best mixed with other types of flour, such as corn if you want to keep it gluten free. Whole hulled buckwheat I use for making porridge.

Oat flakes I use for various kinds of porridge, in raw balls and bread (and as a treat for the hens when the flock is standing in the yard peeking towards the kitchen). Whole hulled oats can be soaked and then blended to make homemade oat milk. Strain it through muslin (cheesecloth) and adjust the flavour with a little salt and possibly some agave syrup.

OILS

Coconut oil is firm at room temperature, when it resembles fats such as butter or dairy-free spread. In Sweden it comes both as warm- or cold-pressed oil, and I like to have both varieties in the cupboard. The cold-pressed oil has a mild coconut flavour, so for occasions when you don't want the food to taste like coconut, warm-pressed oil is a better alternative.

When it comes to liquid oils, cold- and warm-pressed rapeseed (canola) oil as well as olive oil are the ones I always have at home. Olive oil is best for vinaigrettes, dressings and for drizzling over cooked food. Warm- and cold-pressed rapeseed oils are very different in flavour. The warm-pressed oil is completely neutral in flavour and is therefore good to use when you don't want the oil to add any flavour – in mayonnaise for instance – while the cold-pressed oil has a lot of character and a nutty flavour (which can be a bit of an acquired taste) as well as a beautiful golden colour.

FLAVOUR ENHANCERS

Tamari is a gluten-free soy sauce made from fermented soya beans. It gives a deep umami or savoury flavour to many dishes.

Miso, like tamari, is made from fermented soya beans and comes in several different varieties. It has a strong umami flavour and can be used in much the same way as stock. However, do read the label on the packaging to make sure it's vegan.

Tahini is a paste or a seed butter made from sesame seeds, often toasted. It has a rich, nutty flavour that is good in dressings, sauces and hummus. It can also be used as a spread for bread and crackers and is particularly tasty with something sweet, such as sliced banana or other fruit.

Dried mushrooms can be blitzed to a powder in a mini food processor or coffee grinder and used as a stock in soups and stews or as a flavouring for bean burgers if you want to make them richer. They can also be soaked until soft and then fried or added to sauces and stews.

Both sun-dried tomatoes and tomato purée (paste) have a complex flavour with a combination of acidity, sweetness, saltiness and umami.

I always use cider vinegar or lemon juice in my cooking to add acidity.

THE FLAVOURS OF CHRISTMAS

The flavours of Christmas are generally fairly distinctive, which means that you can create a completely new dish that still tastes traditional and classic. In the Scandinavian kitchen, for example, we rarely use saffron as a spice at other times of the year, and spices such as cinnamon, caraway and cardamom are always popular in festive baking. If you bring together these different spices in new and different ways then it's possible to recreate the spirit of Christmas, whether it be at the dinner table or at coffee time.

CITRUS (ORANGES, CLEMENTINES AND BITTER ORANGE): winter is the season for citrus fruit in some parts of the world and it's a time when these sweet-sour fruits are most juicy and at their best. Bitter orange is mostly used at Christmas time as a flavouring, such as in the traditional Swedish wort bread or as a spice for mulled wine. A little grated orange or clementine zest is nice with chocolate as well as in cakes, or simply grated over porridge.

JUNIPER BERRIES: these have a flavour that reminds me of the forest and, more specifically, Christmas trees. The spice is good in burgers and stews or in Christmas crispbreads and tea blends. Juniper berries can be picked all year round in Sweden and are therefore one of the few ingredients that you can pick from nature's own larder during this time of the year.

And speaking about Christmas trees, if you have a real one with roots that's planted in a pot, there's a chance that it will start growing in the warmth of your home and sprout fresh new shoots. These can be used in infusions as long as the tree is organic and hasn't been sprayed with pesticides or herbicides (see page 26).

GINGER (GROUND): a key flavour in classic ginger snap cookies. When fresh, ginger is an unusually aromatic root that is also spicy in flavour.

CINNAMON, CARDAMOM AND CLOVES: these typical ginger snap spices are also found in garam masala and chai. The spices are super delicious in teas, infusions and breads, as well as soups, stews and bakes such as the classic Jansson's temptation (see page 99). The latter doesn't have to contain fish. In the book I give a vegan alternative to the classic creamy, fishy potato gratin featuring a traditional combination of allspice, cloves, cinnamon, bay leaves and ginger.

CARAMEL: knäck (Christmas butterscotch) and other toffees are our most common festive sweets. Dates, coconut sugar and maple syrup also have a distinct caramel flavour.

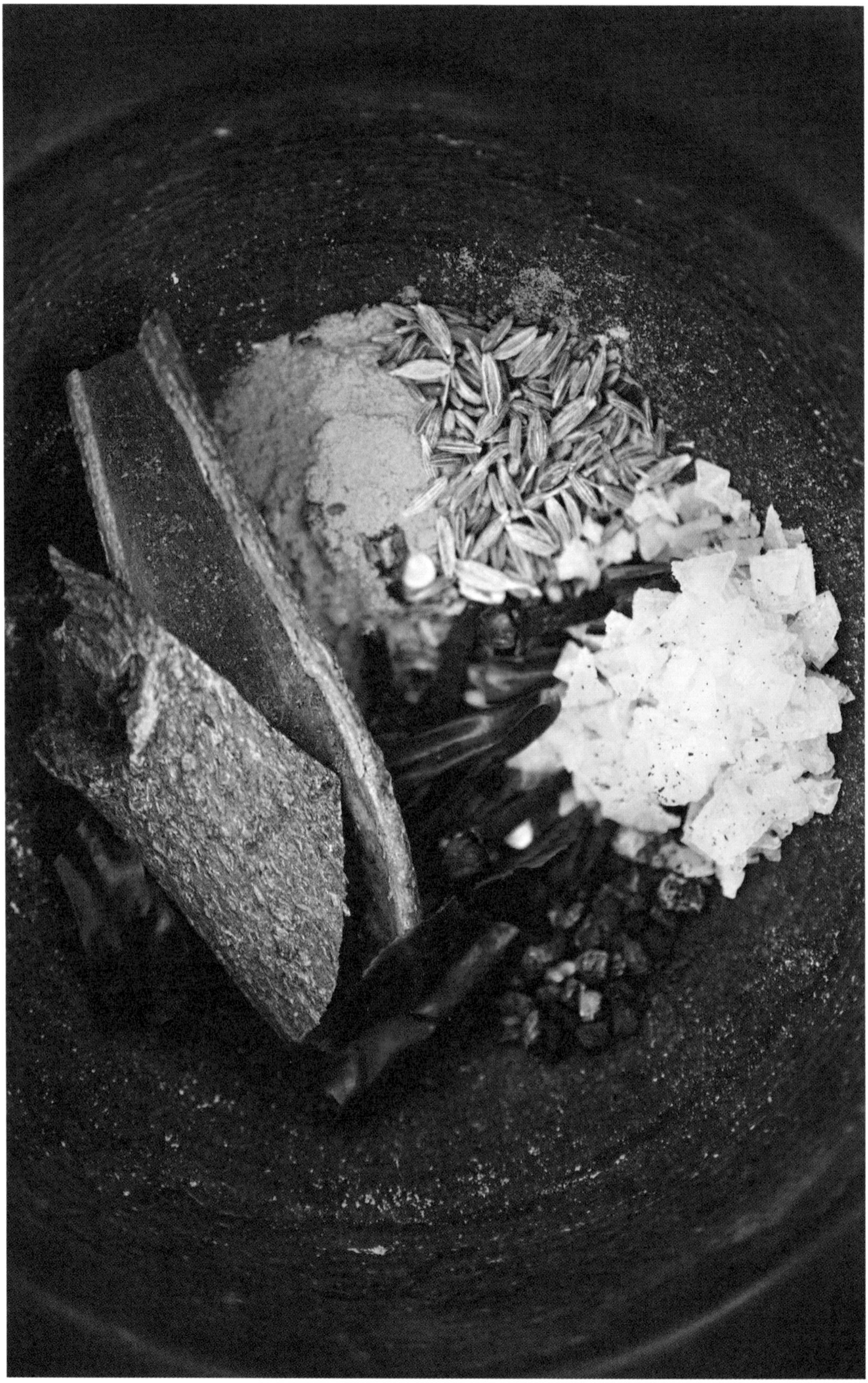

ALLSPICE AND WHITE PEPPER: two pepper varieties that are commonly used in traditional Swedish food and, for me, take me right back in time to my grandma's cabbage rolls or my dad's meatballs.

DRIED FRUIT: figs and dates are particularly associated with Christmas time. Use them in Middle Eastern-style dishes or add to festive sweets and raw food 'baking' as an alternative to sugar.

LINGONBERRIES: these complex-tasting berries have, apart from sweetness and acidity, a distinctive bitterness, that makes them suitable for both sweet and savoury cooking. In other words, lingonberries are just as delicious in caramel as they are in gravy.

NUTS (ALMONDS, WALNUTS, HAZELNUTS AND PISTACHIOS): these are definitely an essential part of Christmas. Pistachios, just like dates, figs and saffron, bring a special Middle Eastern feel to festive dishes. Apart from baking, nuts are great roasted or used as a crunchy topping for salads, soups and porridge.

SMOKED FOODS: historically, smoked foods are very popular in Sweden. It's easier to smoke foods at home than you might think and they make a great addition to a vegan Christmas buffet – smoked beetroot (beets), burgers or balls for instance. A smoky flavour can also be achieved with spices such as chipotle chillies.

BAY LEAVES: these are aromatic and can add depth of flavour to stock and stews.

SAFFRON: in many parts of the world this spice is used to add flavour and colour to dishes such as soups, sauces and stews. In the Swedish kitchen it is probably mostly associated with festive saffron bread. That's why a little saffron added to dinner or in baking means instant Christmas flavour.

MUSTARD: with its combination of slight acidity and sweetness, mustard gives a lovely rounded flavour to gratins, sauces and mayonnaise, and is good mixed into oat cream.

UMAMI: the classic Swedish Christmas buffet is a proper meat feast. The rich, savoury flavour of meat can best be described as umami. If you want to mimic this punchy flavour, umami is the thing to add. Umami in the plant world can be found in ingredients such as sun-dried tomatoes, tomato purée (paste), tahini, bay leaves, cumin, tamari, miso paste, fried onions and mushrooms, roasted nuts and seeds, lovage, celery and nutritional yeast.

WORT: this malt extract is mixed with water and has a fermented malt flavour. It is a popular ingredient in the brewing of beer and adds flavour to Swedish sourdough wort bread.

WINTER CULTIVATION

In winter you can have loads of fun with sprouting; not only is it cultivation in its simplest form, it can be done indoors. My favourite thing to grow is mung bean sprouts as they're cheap, quick, nutritious and give a good yield. They also have a fresh, mild flavour that I find appealing. Other favourites are radish and beetroot (beet) sprouts.

Place 100g/3½oz/scant ½ cup mung bean seeds in a large sterilized jar, cover with cold water and leave to soak overnight at room temperature and away from direct sunlight. The next day, strain off the water and leave the seeds to stand. It's important to remove any excess water so that the seeds don't become too wet and turn mouldy. I usually place a piece of cloth over the opening and turn the jar upside down to remove any excess water.

Rinse the seeds 2–3 times per day. After about 2 days the sprouts will be ready to eat, but you can leave them for 3–5 days – the sprouts will get longer, and eventually grow little leaves and turn into bean shoots. Store the bean shoots in the fridge when sprouted.

SPRUCE SHOOTS

In nature, there are still months to go until the spruce and other coniferous trees start to grow shoots. But the Christmas tree (make sure it's organic), standing in the warmth of the home, can get spring feelings and start sprouting. The new shoots can be made into an infusion, among other things. Place the spruce shoots, a few juniper berries, a crushed piece of fresh ginger, a few cloves and perhaps some lemon in a teapot, pour over hot water and leave to infuse for 5 minutes before straining.

CHRISTMAS FLOWERS

Once Christmas is over, there are a few flowers that you should make the most of and save. Hyacinths, which are actually spring flowers, can be planted out in the garden and will continue to flower year after year. Leave the stem to wilt and then save the bulb until you're able to dig it down into the ground. Also, Christmas rose can be planted out into the flower bed, while the amaryllis bulb can be saved for the following Christmas.

BAKING

MY APPETITE FOR CHRISTMAS baking kicks in around early November. I crave saffron buns, wort bread and ginger snaps. And since the days are short and the evenings long, you end up staying indoors a lot more; it's a perfect time to knead, roll and prove dough and to enjoy freshly baked cakes and bread. In this chapter I have gathered a few of my absolutely favourite recipes, but the list could have been so much longer!

Baking for Christmas is especially lovely in my opinion – it feels like there is a lot of history behind our traditional recipes. The Ginger Snaps recipe (see page 44) is originally my grandmother's and dates back nearly 100 years, while the origins of panforte (see page 53) can be traced back to the 15th century, at least. On my baking sheets, dark as midnight, shine the saffron-yellow Lucia buns, like stars and celestial bodies (see pages 36–37). Shapes such as 'babe-in-arms', 'the vicar's hair', 'Christmas goat', and 'horse and cart' remind me of bygone days in a Sweden built by farming communities. I dig out my old embroidered linen tea (dish) towels made by relatives and use them as warming blankets to drape over raising dough, just like they've been used for over 100 years. Yet, we should not only look backwards. In this chapter, you'll also find new recipes for goodies such as raw carrot balls and cashew ice cream, date pralines and candied orange slices dipped in vegan dark chocolate.

Vegan baking doesn't differ that much from baking with dairy and eggs, but there are occasions when you have to rethink a little and use alternative ingredients in order to get the same result. Eggs are easily replaced in cakes with a little extra liquid and, for example, psyllium husk, which is an efficient binding agent. Chia seeds and chia flour can be used in the same way. You may also have to add a little baking powder or other raising agent. Dairy products can simply be replaced with the equivalent plant-based version. When it comes to fat I think oils are in almost every circumstance superior to firm fats like butter or spreads; they add more moisture to buns and other baked goods and, as a rule, will last for longer.

PAGE 40

CINNAMON AND WALNUT BREAD

{makes 1 loaf}

10g/⅓oz fresh yeast (or about 5g/⅛oz dried)

500g/1lb 2oz/3¾ cups spelt flour, sifted, plus extra for dusting

½ tbsp salt

1 tsp ground cinnamon

70g/2½oz/½ cup walnuts

This is a slow-rise bread just like the carrot bread on page 41. I've eaten cinnamon-spiced bread in Indian restaurants before and think it's a particularly ingenious idea to use this fragrant, aromatic spice for savoury breads, not just for sweet baking like we usually do in Sweden.

The water that you pour into the baking dish when baking the bread turns into steam, which in turn helps to create a lovely crust on the bread. This bread is particularly good toasted, so do try it.

Stir the yeast into 300ml/10½fl oz/generous 1¼ cups cold water in a large mixing bowl until dissolved. Add the flour and salt and work into a dough. Cover the bowl with cling film (plastic wrap) and leave the dough to rise for about 18 hours at room temperature.

Tip the dough out onto a floured work surface and stretch it into a rectangle shape, without pressing out any air. Sprinkle over the cinnamon and the walnuts. Fold the dough a couple of times until it becomes tight, and shape into a round 18cm/7in loaf. Cover with a cloth and leave the dough to prove for 2 hours.

Preheat the oven to 250°C/500°F/Gas 9 and place a heavy-based, ovenproof saucepan (with a heatproof handle) in the oven to heat up, as well as a deep baking dish in the bottom.

Carefully, put the dough in the hot pan and place it in the oven. Pour 100ml/3½fl oz/generous ⅓ cup water into the baking dish and close the oven door. Lower the heat to 200°C/400°F/Gas 6 after 10 minutes and bake the bread for around 50 minutes or until risen and golden.

Leave to cool slightly, then turn the loaf out of the pan and leave to cool completely on a wire rack.

{makes 2 loaves}

3½ tbsp rapeseed (canola) oil

500ml/17fl oz/generous 2 cups porter, svagdricka or julmust

½ tbsp ground bitter orange peel

1 tbsp ground ginger

1 tsp ground cloves

50g/1¾oz fresh yeast (or about 25g/1oz dried)

2½ tbsp brown sugar

1 tbsp soy sauce

800g/1lb 12oz/5¾ cups spelt flour, sifted

100g/3½oz/¾ cup raisins

1 tbsp salt

{makes 2 loaves}

Stage 1:

350g/12oz/2½ cups wholemeal rye flour, sifted

½ tbsp salt

¾ tbsp crushed caraway seeds

Stage 2:

35g/1¼oz fresh yeast (or about 17g/⅔oz dried)

280g/10oz/heaped 2 cups wholemeal or rye flour, sifted

7½ tbsp black treacle

225g/8oz/heaped 1½ cups rye flour, sifted

250g/9oz/scant 2 cups plain (all-purpose) flour, sifted

VÖRTBRÖD / WORT BREAD

It wouldn't be Christmas without wort bread on my table! I usually freeze one loaf for the Christmas buffet too. The ale adds a dark colour and richness to the dough.

~~~~~~~~~~

Heat the oil, porter, orange peel and spices in a pan until tepid. Crumble the yeast into a mixing bowl and pour over the liquid. Stir in the sugar and soy sauce. Work in the flour and raisins. Add the salt and knead the dough a little more, about 5 minutes. Cover and leave to rise for 1 hour or until doubled in size. Shape into two loaves and place in loaf tins (pans). Leave to prove for 2 hours.

Preheat the oven to 200°C/400°F/Gas 6. Bake the loaves for 50 minutes until risen and crusty. If they colour too quickly, cover them with baking parchment. Turn the loaves out onto a wire rack to cool.

KAVRING / DARK RYE BREAD

This bread is milder in flavour than the wort bread, above.

~~~~~~~~~~

Put the rye flour, salt and caraway in a mixing bowl. Bring 500ml/17fl oz/generous 2 cups water to the boil and pour it over the ingredients, stir until mixed well. Cover the bowl and leave to stand overnight.

Heat 250ml/9fl oz/generous 1 cup water to 37°C/98°F and dissolve the yeast in the liquid in a large bowl. Stir in the wholemeal or rye flour and the dough mixture. Cover and leave to rise for 4 hours. Stir in the treacle and the remaining flour and work the dough thoroughly (add more flour if it feels too wet). Shape into two loaves and place in loaf tins (pans). Leave to prove for 2 hours.

Preheat the oven to 180°C/350°F/Gas 4. Bake the loaves for 50 minutes with a baking tray covering the two tins, until risen and crusty. Turn the loaves out to cool.

Dough

250ml/9fl oz/generous
1 cup oat milk, plus
extra for brushing

100ml/3½fl oz/generous
⅓ cup rapeseed (canola) oil

1 tsp cardamom seeds (can
be omitted if you're making
saffron buns without a filling)

1 pinch saffron

90g/3¼oz/scant ½ cup
granulated sugar (or
coconut sugar)

35g/1¼oz fresh yeast (or
about 17g/⅔oz dried)

550g/1lb 4oz/4¼ cups
plain (all-purpose) flour,
plus extra for dusting

1 pinch salt

raisins and pearl (nibbed)
sugar (optional)

Filling (optional)

1 apple, peeled, cored
and roughly chopped

100g/3½oz/¾ cup almonds

5 tbsp coconut oil

70g/2½oz/⅓ cup granulated
sugar (or coconut sugar)

1 tsp crushed cardamom seeds

50–100g/1¾–3½oz/
⅓–¾ cup raisins

SAFFRANSBRÖD / SAFFRON BREAD

Saffron bread, more specifically Lucia buns, are traditionally eaten on December 13th when Swedes celebrate the festival of St. Lucia.

Heat the oat milk and oil to 37°C/98°F in a large pan. Using a pestle and mortar, crush the cardamom seeds and saffron with a little of the sugar.

Crumble the yeast into the liquid, add the spices and sugar and stir until the yeast has dissolved. Add the flour and salt and work into a dough. Leave to rise for 1 hour in a warm place or until doubled in size.

To make the filling, if using, blend together all the ingredients, except the raisins, in a food processor to make a coarse paste. Stir the raisins into the mixture.

LUSSEBULLAR/LUCIA BUNS WITHOUT FILLING (MAKES 15) See photograph, page 28: Turn the risen dough out onto a lightly floured surface and divide into 15 pieces. Roll out one piece of dough into a long, thin sausage, then roll up one end to the middle. Turn over and roll up the other end to the middle to form an S-shape. Press a raisin in each end. Repeat to make 15. Place on a tray lined with baking parchment to prove/bake (see right).

SHAPING

STARS (MAKES 2): Divide the risen dough into 6 even-sized pieces. Roll each piece into a ball and then roll out three of the balls into even-sized rounds. Spread the filling onto one of the rounds, place another round on top. Repeat with the filling and place a third round on top and even out the edges with your hands or a knife.

Mark the middle using a glass, pressing it down halfway. Using a knife, make eight even cuts from the central circle. In the middle of each section, make a long cut. Take the end of the section and thread it through the cut from below, repeat once so that the dough is looped through twice. Repeat with the remaining sections. Place the star on a tray lined with baking parchment to prove/bake (see below). Repeat to make a second star.

LOAVES (MAKES 2): Divide the risen dough in half. Roll each half out into a thin rectangle and spread the filling on top. Roll the dough up, starting from the short edge to make a thick, short roll. Cut the roll in half lengthwise, but leave a join in one end so that the two halves are still attached. Turn the halves so that the cut side is facing upwards and then twist the two halves around each other. Press down on the loaf slightly once twisted and place on a tray lined with baking parchament or in a loaf tin to prove/bake (see below). Repeat with the second roll.

BUNS (MAKES ABOUT 25): Divide the risen dough in half. Roll each half out into a thin rectangle and spread the filling on top. Fold the dough in half and then cut into strips (2–3cm/¾–1in wide). Twist and roll or knot the strips into buns. Place on a tray lined with baking parchment to prove/bake (see below).

PROVING/BAKING

Cover the shaped breads with a tea (dish) towel and prove for 30 minutes. Brush the tops with oat milk and sprinkle with pearl sugar, if using. The stars and loaves are baked at 200°C/400°F/Gas 6 for 20 minutes; the buns at 225°C/425°F/Gas 7 for 10–12 minutes or until risen and golden. Leave to cool on a wire rack covered with a tea (dish) towel.

RUSKS: Cut slightly stale saffron bread into thin slices. Place on a sheet lined with baking parchment and bake at 100°C/200°F/Gas ½ for 1 hour until crisp. Turn off the heat and leave the rusks to dry in the residual heat.

SAFFRANSBRÖD/SAFFRON BREAD - SAFFRON RUSKS

CINNAMON AND WALNUT BREAD - SPICY CARROT BREAD

SPICY CARROT BREAD

BAKING

{makes 1 loaf}

10g/⅓oz fresh yeast (or about 5g/⅛oz dried)

500g/1lb 2oz/3¾ cups spelt flour, sifted, plus extra for dusting

1 carrot, finely grated

finely grated zest of 1 lemon

½ tbsp salt

½ tsp ground fennel

½ tsp ground aniseed

½ tsp ground caraway

I love slow-rise bread! This one takes almost 24 hours from the time the dough is mixed until the loaf is taken out of the oven. But it's well worth the wait: the bread becomes more aromatic and the crumb fluffy as well as delightfully chewy in the same way a sourdough loaf can be. The bread is nice just as it is, but I've chosen to share two completely different flavourings that I think are delicious: carrot, lemon and spice as well as cinnamon and walnut (see page 32).

The carrot bread is flavoured with a favourite mix of spices that I came across several years ago in an Indian restaurant and I've since returned to again and again.

Stir the yeast into 300ml/10½fl oz/generous 1¼ cups cold water in a large mixing bowl until dissolved. Add the flour, carrot, lemon zest, salt and spices and work into a dough. Cover the bowl with cling film (plastic wrap) and leave the dough to rise for about 18 hours at room temperature, until doubled in size.

Tip the dough out onto a floured work surface and stretch it into a rectangle shape, without pressing out any air. Fold the dough a couple of times and shape into a round loaf, about 18cm/7in. Cover with a cloth and leave the dough to prove for 2 hours.

Preheat the oven to 250°C/500°F/Gas 9 and place a 18cm/7in heavy-based pan (with a heatproof handle) in the oven to heat up, as well as a deep baking dish in the bottom.

Carefully, put the dough in the hot pan and place it in the oven. Pour 100ml/3½fl oz/generous ⅓ cup water into the dish and close the oven door. Lower the heat to 200°C/400°F/Gas 6 after 10 minutes and bake the bread for around 50 minutes or until risen and golden.

Leave to cool slightly, then turn the loaf out of the pan and leave to cool completely on a wire rack.

PAGE 43

NO-KNEED SEED CRISPBREADS

{makes about 25}

210g/7½oz/heaped 1½ cups wholemeal spelt flour

8 tbsp unhulled sesame seeds, plus extra for sprinkling (optional)

6 tbsp sunflower seeds

4 tbsp linseeds

4 tbsp chia seeds

1 tsp baking powder

½ tsp salt

1 tsp dried rosemary

1 tbsp olive oil

42
—
43

Occasionally, you just want something home-baked without the need to knead, wait for the dough to rise and scrub off stubborn bits of dough from the work surface. For those occasions, this crispbread recipe is perfect. The dough is loose enough to spread out directly onto baking parchment, so you won't be in need of either a rolling pin or arm muscles to make these crispbreads. I like to flavour the dough with dried rosemary, but caraway, poppy seeds or aniseed could replace the herb just as well.

Preheat the oven to 150°C/300F/Gas 2. Line a baking sheet with baking parchment.

Mix the dry ingredients together in a mixing bowl, add the oil and 250ml/17fl oz/generous 2 cups water and stir into a loose dough. Spread the mixture out in an even layer onto the prepared baking sheet, covering the whole surface. Sprinkle with some more sesame seeds, if you like.

Bake for 45 minutes until crisp and golden. If you want even-sized crispbreads, take them out of the oven after 20 minutes, cut into small pieces and return them to the oven for another 25 minutes until crisp and golden. Alternatively, snap the crispbreads into pieces once baked. Leave to cool on a wire rack.

NO-KNEAD SEED CRISPBREADS

PAGE 46

PEPPARKAKOR / GINGER SNAPS

{makes about 50}

200g/7oz/1 cup brown sugar

3½ tbsp golden syrup (light corn syrup)

1 tbsp ground ginger

½ tsp ground bitter orange peel

1 tbsp ground cinnamon

½ tbsp ground cloves

½ tsp cognac (optional)

125g/4½oz/½ cup plus 1 tbsp dairy-free spread

450g/1lb/scant 3½ cups plain (all-purpose) flour, plus extra for dusting

½ tbsp bicarbonate of soda (baking soda)

This recipe I found in my grandmother's little yellowing recipe collection from the 1930s and 40s, but in her recipe the batch was double the size and not as spicy. For a family celebration like Christmas, I think it's particularly fun to use old family recipes because in a way grandmother Greta, who passed away in the 1960s, is then still present. In the same way, great-grandmother Hilda's old linen cloth with the initials HP, since she kept her maiden name Pålsson, now gets the honourable task to act as a proving cloth for the Christmas breads and buns.

Put the sugar, syrup and 5 tablespoons water in a pan and bring to the boil. Stir in the spices and cognac, if using.

Pour the hot liquid over the spread in a mixing bowl and stir until it has melted, then leave to cool. Add the flour and bicarbonate of soda and beat with a wooden spoon into a smooth dough. Leave the dough to rest in a cool place until the next day.

Preheat the oven to 225°C/425°F/Gas 7 and line a baking sheet with baking parchment.

Cut the dough in half and roll out each half thinly on a lightly floured work surface. Cut out shapes with a cookie cutter and move to the lined baking sheet using a dough scraper or spatula. Bake in the middle of the oven for 5 minutes or until golden and crisp. Place on a wire rack to cool before icing (see right), if you like.

PAGE 47

ICING

125g/4½oz/scant 1 cup icing (confectioners') sugar, sifted

1½ tbsp lemon juice or water

Icing made with lemon juice is more acidic in flavour and becomes a little harder and whiter than if you make it with water, but you could also do a 50:50 mix of lemon and water.

Mix the icing sugar into the lemon juice or water in a bowl until you've got a good consistency for piping – add more icing sugar if it is too runny. If it's too thick, on the other hand, add more lemon juice or water, a drop at a time. Try piping a little of the icing and adjust the amount of liquid or icing sugar, if necessary.

To use, fill the piping bag and close the opening with a freezer bag clip so that the icing doesn't escape through the top when you start piping. Cut a small hole in the tip for piping – a tiny opening is the best, so start small and then cut a little more if you need a larger hole.

The piping bags can be washed up afterwards to use again if you like.

PEPPARKAKOR / GINGER SNAPS - ICING

GINGER CAKE WITH LINGONBERRIES

{makes 1 cake}

Cake

100ml/3½fl oz/generous
⅓ cup rapeseed (canola) oil,
plus extra for greasing

dried breadcrumbs, for coating

90g/3¼oz/scant ½ cup
granulated sugar (or you could
use brown or coconut sugar)

210g/7½oz/heaped
1½ cups spelt flour, sifted

2 tsp bicarbonate of
soda (baking soda)

1½ tsp ground cinnamon

1 tsp crushed cardamom seeds

1 tsp ground cloves

1 tsp ground ginger

200ml/7fl oz/generous
¾ cup oat milk

6½ tbsp lingonberry jam

icing (confectioners') sugar,
sifted, for dusting (optional)

Frosting (optional)

140g/5oz/heaped
1 cup cashew nuts

5 soft dates, pitted

½ tsp vanilla powder

finely grated zest of
1 lemon and juice of
½ lemon

When I started to bake without dairy products and egg, this cake was the first one I made and it's still one of my favourites. It's literally a piece of cake to throw together, is packed with lovely Christmas spices, and keeps nice and moist for many days.

Here, I have decorated the cake with a dusting of icing (confectioners') sugar: simply place a doily on top of the cake and sift over the icing sugar to create a beautiful pattern. If you want to make it even more festive, top with the delicious cashew nut frosting, below.

~~~~~~~~~~~~~~~~~~~~~~~~~~~~~~~~

To make the frosting, if using, soak the cashew nuts for at least 5 hours in water until softened, then drain. Put the nuts, dates, vanilla powder, lemon zest and juice and 100ml/3½fl oz/generous ⅓ cup water in a high-speed blender and blend until smooth. Add a little more water if the consistency is too thick. Set aside.

Preheat the oven to 180°C/350°F/Gas 4. Grease and coat a 20cm/8in cake tin (pan) with breadcrumbs.

Mix together all the dry ingredients in a mixing bowl. Whisk in the oat milk and oil and finally stir in the lingonberry jam.

Pour the batter into the prepared cake tin. Bake for 35 minutes or until a skewer comes out dry when inserted in the middle of the cake. Leave the cake to sit for 5 minutes before turning it out of the tin. Leave to cool on a wire rack.

Spread the frosting, if using, over the cake once it has fully cooled, or dust with icing sugar.

SCONES WITH ORANGE, CRANBERRY AND ALMOND

SCONES WITH ORANGE, CRANBERRY AND ALMOND

{makes 1 large round}

210g/7½oz/heaped
1½ cups spelt flour, sifted

finely grated zest of ½ orange

4 tbsp dried cranberries

2½ tsp baking powder

½ tsp salt

50g/1¾oz/4 tbsp dairy-free
spread or coconut oil

150ml/5fl oz/⅔ cup oat milk

flaked almonds, to decorate

I love British fruit scones and this is my Christmas take on them, flavoured with cranberry and orange. They're quick to make since they don't need to rise and only take 15 minutes in the oven – perfect for serving on dark advent mornings.

~~~~~~~~~~~~~~~~~~~~~~~~~~~~~~~~~~

Preheat the oven to 250°C/500°F/Gas 9. Line a baking sheet with baking parchment.

Mix together the flour, orange zest, cranberries, baking powder and salt in a mixing bowl. Rub the fat into the flour using your fingertips. Add the milk and quickly work into a dough.

Wet your hands and shape the dough into a round. Place on the prepared baking sheet, flatten the top slightly and sprinkle with flaked almonds. Score a cross into the dough to mark it into four pieces. Bake for 15 minutes or until risen and golden. Leave to cool slightly on a wire rack.

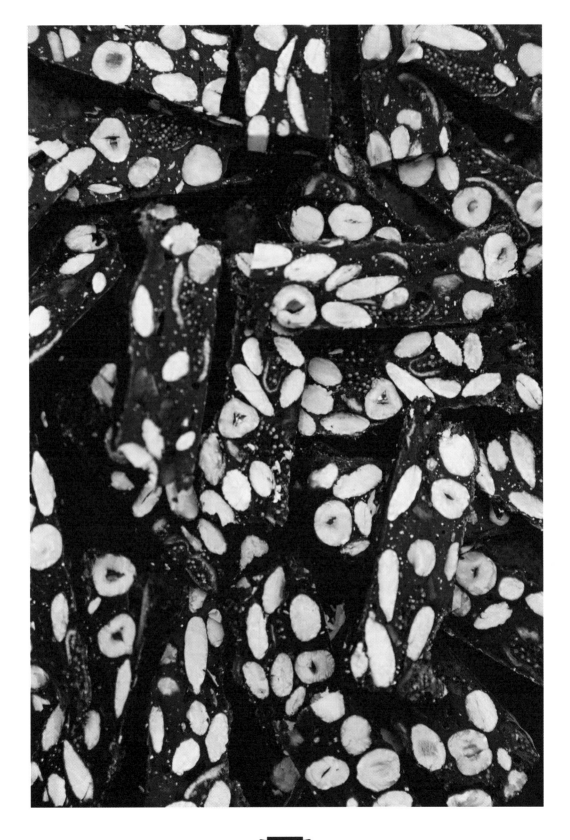

PANFORTE

PAGE 52

PANFORTE

{makes 1}

250g/9oz/2 cups mixed nuts, such as hazelnuts and almonds

70g/2½oz/½ cup plain (all-purpose) flour

150g/5½oz/1 cup chopped dried figs

finely grated zest of 1 orange

1½ tsp crushed cardamom seeds

½ tsp salt

5 tbsp agave syrup

70g/2½oz/⅓ cup coconut sugar

100g/3½oz vegan dark chocolate (70% cacao), broken into pieces

icing (confectioners') sugar, for dusting

This nut-packed chocolate cake is something of a personal favourite because it has a wonderful chewy texture and is packed with Christmas flavours. Panforte is usually flavoured with cloves, cinnamon, nutmeg and aniseed, but I flavour mine with orange zest and freshly crushed cardamon seeds instead – a flavour combination that I think works fantastically with the chocolate, figs and roasted nuts. I like to serve it cut into thin slices with a cup of coffee.

Roast the nuts in a large, dry frying pan (skillet) until starting to colour. Rub off any loose skin using a clean, dry tea (dish) towel.

In a mixing bowl, mix the nuts with the flour, figs, orange zest, cardamom and salt. Set aside.

Pour the syrup and sugar into a pan and heat gently until the sugar has melted. Add the chocolate and stir until the chocolate has melted. Pour the mixture over the nuts and stir until thoroughly combined.

Preheat the oven to 170°C/325°F/Gas 3. Spoon the mixture into a 20cm/8in springform cake tin (pan) lined with baking parchment and press out evenly using a slightly dampened hand. Bake for 18–20 minutes until the surface of the cake is dry but springy when pressed.

Leave the cake to cool in the tin, then remove the baking parchment. Sprinkle the top with icing sugar and rub it into the cake with your hand. Cut into thin slices.

PAGE 56

{makes 350g/12oz/
3¾ cups}

1½ tbsp sugar of your
choice, such as granulated,
brown or coconut sugar

2 tbsp tamari

1 tbsp olive oil

1–2 tsp dried rosemary

350g/12oz/
3¾ cups mixed nuts
(or seeds if you like)

SWEET 'N' SALTY MIXED NUTS

Candied almonds are a winter classic in Sweden. Here, I've decreased the amount of sugar and instead made them a little sweet-salty by adding tamari. These nuts are really quick to make, but watch them carefully in the oven, they can burn before you know it!

Preheat the oven to 170°C/325°F/Gas 3.

In a bowl, mix together the sugar, tamari, olive oil and rosemary.

Put the nuts on a baking sheet and toast for 5 minutes in the oven.

Tip the nuts into a bowl, pour over the olive oil mixture and stir until everything is thoroughly mixed.

Return the nuts to the baking sheet, spread them out evenly and toast for a further 5–7 minutes until golden.

HALF MOONS

{makes 20}

3 thin-skinned organic oranges (it's especially important to use organic)

100ml/3½fl oz/generous ⅓ cup agave syrup

100g/3½oz vegan dark chocolate, preferably with a cocoa content between 55–60% (the sweetness is needed to counteract the bitterness of the orange peel)

It feels rather symbolic to make these bittersweet chocolate-orange slices when the midwinter darkness lies like a black blanket over our northern hemisphere, with short days, dark nights and scarcity of light. So when I was thinking of a name for this treat, they had to embody that feeling of midwinter darkness and solar and lunar eclipse – I decided to name them half moons.

Wash and thinly slice the oranges into rounds. Mix 150ml/5fl oz/⅔ cup water with the syrup in a large bowl. Add the oranges and stir to coat them in the liquid. Leave to stand overnight or for about 8 hours at room temperature.

Preheat the oven to its lowest setting. Remove the orange slices from the liquid, let them drain a little and then place on a tray lined with baking parchment. Put the oranges in the oven to dry, turning them over from time to time to keep them flat. You can also open the oven door occasionally to release any steam. The drying will take about 12 hours.

Melt half of the chocolate over a bain-marie or in a heatproof bowl placed over a pan of gently simmering water. Finely chop the remaining chocolate. When the chocolate has melted, remove the bowl from the heat, add the remaining chopped chocolate and stir until everything has melted.

Dip the orange slices halfway into the melted chocolate so only one half is coated. Leave to set on a tray lined with baking parchment.

MIXED NUTS - HALF MOONS

PAGE 60

{makes 15–20}

100g/3½oz vegan dark chocolate (70% cacao), broken into pieces

15–20 soft dates, pitted

about 7 tbsp almond butter (shop bought or see below)

finely chopped almonds or cacao nibs (optional)

DATE PRALINES

These date pralines are absolutely incredible: they are simple to make, only require three ingredients and are magically delicious, creamy and irresistible.

Melt half of the chocolate over a bain-marie or in a heatproof bowl placed over a pan of gently simmering water. Meanwhile, finely chop the remaining chocolate. Remove the melted chocolate from the heat and add the chopped chocolate, stir until everything has melted.

Fill each date with a dollop of almond butter. Pinch the top of the date to encase the filling and dip it into the melted chocolate. Leave to dry on a tray lined with baking parchment and repeat with the remaining dates, filling and chocolate.

If you want to make the pralines extra fancy, sprinkle finely chopped almonds over the top before the chocolate sets. Cacao nibs are another great topping.

ALMOND BUTTER

To make your own almond butter: roast 140g/5oz/scant 1 cup almonds in a dry frying pan (skillet) until lightly coloured, then blend in a food processor until smooth and creamy. This requires a fairly powerful machine, but blending can be made easier by mixing the almonds with a little oil. Season to taste with a little salt.

CHOCOLATE FUDGE WITH SEA BUCKTHORN AND WALNUTS

This is a bit like a hybrid between truffles and fudge. It's not as dry and sugary as some fudge can be, but remains creamy and smooth like a truffle. It's no surprise then that it's one of the big Christmas sweet favourites at home and rarely lasts very long.

The dried sea buckthorn powder can be replaced with blueberry, lingonberry or cranberry powder, which are made in the same way (see below), or can be bought online.

{makes about 25}

100ml/3½fl oz/generous ⅓ cup coconut oil

100ml/3½fl oz/generous ⅓ cup dark syrup, such as date or muscovado syrup

3½ tbsp oat cream

100g/3½oz vegan dark chocolate (70% cacao), broken into pieces

3½ tbsp cacao powder

a few pinches of salt

100g/3½oz/⅔ cup walnut halves

2 tbsp dried sea buckthorn powder (see right), or dried blueberry, lingonberry or cranberry powder

Mix together the coconut oil, syrup and oat cream in a pan and heat gently until simmering. Remove from the heat and add the chocolate. Stir until the chocolate has melted, then mix in the cacao, salt and walnuts. If you prefer, break the nuts into smaller pieces before you stir them in.

Line a 17 x 12cm (6½ x 4½in) dish with baking parchment or cling film (plastic wrap) and pour in the fudge mixture, then place in the fridge to set. Sprinkle over the sea buckthorn powder, or other fruit powder, when the chocolate is still a little sticky. Leave to set completely and cut into cubes.

SEA BUCKTHORN POWDER

When I make sea buckthorn juice I save the pulp to dry it into a powder. To make your own, either juice 400g/14oz/ scant 3 cups sea buckthorn berries, or place the berries and 100ml/3½fl oz/generous ⅓ cup water in a blender and blend to a purée. Strain through a piece of muslin (cheesecloth) and squeeze out all the juice. Spread the pulp in the cloth onto a piece of baking parchment and dry in the oven on the lowest setting, or in a dehydrator. Once dried, you'll have a fresh and slightly zingy powder to use as a flavouring and/or for decoration.

BAKING

DATE PRALINES - CHOCOLATE FUDGE WITH SEA BUCKTHORN AND WALNUTS

PAGE 63

CARROT BALLS WITH LEMON AND CARDAMOM

{makes about 15}

1 carrot, about 150g/5½oz, finely grated

finely grated zest of 1 lemon

10 soft dates, pitted and roughly chopped

100g/3½oz/¾ cup rolled porridge oats

3½ tbsp coconut oil

2 pinches of crushed cardamom seeds

ground cinnamon, for dusting (optional)

Christmas time can often bring a lot of stress, travelling and running around here and there. These raw food balls are packed with good energy and are perfect for bringing as a snack on a journey to relatives, or for a winter's day out.

Place all the ingredients in a mixing bowl and blend using a stick blender to a smooth mixture.

Roll the mixture into walnut-sized balls and leave to stand in the fridge for at least 1 hour. Dust the balls with cinnamon, if you like.

ICE CREAM POPS WITH CINNAMON AND SEA BUCKTHORN

BAKING

{makes 8}

Ice cream

140g/5oz/scant 1 cup cashew nuts

200g/7oz/scant 1½ cups sea buckthorn berries or berry of your choice

100ml/3½fl oz/generous ⅓ cup oat cream

3½ tbsp agave syrup

1 tbsp coconut oil

2 tsp lemon juice

1 tsp ground cinnamon

Topping

80g/2¾oz vegan white chocolate, broken into pieces

cacao nibs, freeze-dried strawberries and dried lingonberry powder, or your choice

Do you fancy ice cream in the winter? Of course! This one I've flavoured with sea buckthorn berries and cinnamon, but if you'd like to vary the flavour, you could try frozen strawberries and vanilla, or blueberries and cardamom instead – imagination is the only limit. Don't forget to top the ice pops with all sorts of goodies.

Soak the cashew nuts in water for at least 5 hours until softened. Strain off the soaking water and place the nuts with the other ice cream ingredients in a blender, preferably a high-speed one. Blend everything until completely smooth and creamy. Pour the mixture into 8 small ice lolly moulds, insert sticks and freeze.

When the ice cream lollies are thoroughly frozen, remove them from their moulds and place on a piece of baking parchment.

Melt the chocolate in a bain-marie or heatproof bowl placed over a pan of gently simmering water. Drizzle a little of the melted chocolate over one of the ice cream pops and quickly sprinkle with toppings, such as cacao nibs, strawberries and lingonberry powder. Repeat with the remaining ice cream lollies until you've topped all of them. Since the ice cream is so cold, the chocolate will set quickly, so it's best to top them one at a time.

ÆBLESKIVER/DANISH PANCAKE PUFFS

ÆBLESKIVER / DANISH PANCAKE PUFFS

{makes about 14}

210g/7½oz/heaped 1½ cups plain (all-purpose) flour, sifted

2–3 tbsp coconut sugar (or other sugar)

2 tsp baking powder

1 pinch crushed cardamom seeds

200ml/7fl oz/generous ¾ cup oat milk

2 tbsp rapeseed (canola) oil, plus extra for greasing

icing (confectioners') sugar, for dusting

Apple sauce

1 apple, peeled, cored and roughly chopped

1½ tsp ground cinnamon

When I was growing up, there was a frying pan (skillet) tucked away in the pan cupboard with deep, round indentations that confused me a great deal. It was pretty much never used. My mum called it a 'doughnut pan', but for me a doughnut was significantly larger than what could be cooked in this pan. It was, of course, an æbleskiver pan and this Danish treat is a bit like a filled pancake doughnut.

I actually use the exact same recipe for æbleskiver as I do for American pancakes and I fill them with a raw apple sauce. Apple isn't actually an obligatory ingredient in æbleskiver, even though it certainly sounds like it from the name. In Denmark, æbleskiver are eaten around Christmas time in particular, but I think it's a rather festive way to fry pancakes for a weekend breakfast at any time of the year.

BAKING

~~~~~~~~~~~~~~~~~~~~~~~~

Mix together the dry ingredients in a mixing bowl until thoroughly combined. Add the oat milk and oil and whisk to remove any lumps of flour.

Place the apple in a bowl. Add the cinnamon and 2–3 tablespoons water and blend until fairly smooth.

Heat the æbleskiver pan, grease the indentations with oil and add a dollop of batter so that each one is coated. Add a teaspoon of the apple sauce to each one and then cover with a little more pancake batter. Fry until the æbleskiver start to brown around the edges. Use a skewer to turn them over and fry for 1–2 minutes on the other side until coloured nicely. Dust with icing sugar before serving.

BIRCH ADVENT CANDLEHOLDER

Beauty can often be found in the simple, and if you want to make your own advent candleholder in the simplest and cheapest way then this one in birchwood is perfect. I used a birch branch/log about 15cm/6in diameter and 30cm/12in long, then I cut it almost in half lengthwise through the middle.

You can use a handsaw to cut the log, or place an axe where you want to make the cut and then knock it out using a log or mallet so that the branch splits. If you use an axe, you may need to even it out a with a handplane afterwards to make sure the candleholder stands flat on the table.

To make a place for the candles, drill four holes using a 2cm/¾in drill bit. Measure the holes before you start drilling, so that they are evenly spaced.

If you then want to go all the way, add pine cones, lichen, cinnamon sticks and dried orange slices for decoration, gluing them to the birch log.

It's as simple as that to make this candleholder in a beautiful natural material. If you don't have any birch at hand you can, of course, use other types of wood.

DRINKS

{makes about 1.5
litres/50fl oz/6¼ cups}

1 tbsp juniper berries

1 tsp whole cloves

2 star anise

800g/1lb 12oz/8 heaped
cups sloe berries

3 cinnamon sticks

100g/3½oz/½ cup
granulated sugar (or brown
or coconut sugar)

MULLED SLOE DRINK

*Apart from juniper berries, sloes are probably the berries that
can be picked the latest in the year where I live in Sweden – it's
normally around advent that I get out to pick them. Stored
ingredients are all very well and good, but there is an extra special
charm to being outdoors and foraging for Christmas foods, while
your cheeks turn red from the cold. And the moment when you
huddle around the fire and sip on your homemade mulled sloe
drink, made from what nature has to offer, is close to magic.*

~~~~~~~~~~~~~~~~~~~~~~

Roughly crush the juniper berries, cloves and star anise
using a pestle and mortar. Put the sloe berries, cinnamon
sticks and the crushed spices in a large, heatproof bowl.

Bring 1.5 litres/50fl oz/6¼ cups water to the boil in a
pan and pour it over the spices and berries in the bowl.
Leave to cool, then strain the liquid through a mesh sieve
(fine strainer) into the pan.

Return the sloe berries and spices to the bowl and
bring the liquid to the boil again. Pour it over the mixture
in the bowl and leave to cool once more.

Repeat a further three times, adding the sugar the last
time you heat the liquid. Strain through muslin and let
all the liquid drip through without squeezing it out. Taste
and add more sugar, if needed. Heat your mulled sloe
drink before serving.

CHAGA CHAICCINO

PAGE 75

{serves 1}

100ml/3½fl oz/generous
⅓ cup oat milk, plus extra
to serve (optional)

1 tsp agave syrup

½ tsp chaga powder

½ tsp ground cinnamon

½ tsp ground ginger

1 pinch crushed
cardamom seeds

1 tsp ground cloves

*Chaga is a type of mushroom and can be bought as a powder
in health food stores. It doesn't taste of much so I've paired it with
classic aromatic chai spices, such as cinnamon, ginger, cardamom
and cloves. Have a lie in and curl up in bed with a warming cup
of chaga chaiccino!*

Mix all the ingredients with 100ml/3½fl oz/generous
⅓ cup water in a pan. Heat until it's simmering, then
pour into a glass or a cup. For a frothy topping, foam a
little extra milk and pour over.

GOLDEN MILK

PAGE 75

{serves 1}

100ml/3½fl oz/generous
⅓ cup oat milk, plus extra
to serve (optional)

1 piece fresh turmeric,
about 1 x 1cm/½ x ½in

1 piece fresh ginger,
about 2 x 2cm/¾ x ¾in

1 tsp agave syrup

½ tsp ground cinnamon

*If I come down with a cold or catch a fever during winter,
golden milk is the best drink I know, and it tastes lovely –
a refreshing combination of ginger and turmeric. It doesn't just
warm you thanks to the temperature of the drink, but also
because of the spices. A perfect health booster!*

Place all the ingredients with 100ml/3½fl oz/generous
⅓ cup water in a blender (you don't need to peel the
turmeric and ginger), then blend until smooth and pour
into a pan. Heat to 60°C/140°F, then strain through
a mesh sieve (fine strainer) or tea strainer into a glass
or cup. For a frothy topping, foam a little extra milk
and pour over.

MULLED SLOE DRINK · CHAGA CHAICCINO · GOLDEN MILK

MIDVINTERBLOT SHOT

{makes about 500ml/
17fl oz/generous 2 cups}

2 raw beetroot (beets),
about 200g/7oz total
weight, scrubbed and
cut into small pieces

1 blood orange, peeled

1 lemon, peeled

100g/3½oz fresh ginger,
peeled

50g/1¾oz fresh
turmeric, unpeeled

For some reason it feels extra important to eat and drink a lot of colourful foods when you feel at your palest self, and the weather is constantly grey and wet. This Christmas shot is packed with colourful and nutritious ingredients that boost your body during this barren, tough time.

The name of the shot translates as 'midwinter sacrifice'. This comes, of course, from its intensely red colour, which bears a resemblance to blood and the sacrifices that took place in the ancient Nordics around Christmas. But don't worry, this is as bloody as it gets in the plant-based kitchen!

Place all the ingredients and 200ml/7fl oz/generous ¾ cup water in a blender, preferably a high-speed one, and blend until smooth. Strain through muslin and squeeze out all the juice. You can also strain the juice through a mesh sieve (fine strainer), but if you do the juice may split.

MIDVINTERBLOT SHOT

HOT CHOCOLATE

{serves 1}

200ml/7fl oz/generous ¾ cup oat milk, plus extra to serve (optional)

1 tbsp cacao powder

½ tbsp agave syrup

1 tsp tahini

1 pinch chilli powder or ground cinnamon (optional)

HOT CHOCOLATE

A winter picnic would be incomplete without a large thermos filled with hot chocolate. I add a little tahini to mine, which gives a rounder and slightly nutty flavour. If you'd like a bit of extra heat, add a pinch of chilli powder – it's believed that the Mayans added it to their chocolate drinks thousands of years ago.

Put all the ingredients in a pan and whisk to dissolve the cacao powder. Heat until simmering, then pour it into a glass or cup. For a frothy topping, foam a little extra milk and pour over.

PAGE 82

{makes 2 litres/68fl oz/8½ cups}

4 chai tea bags

1 orange or blood orange, preferably organic, cut into small pieces

COLD BREW CHAI

Cold brew tea is a tasty alternative to the sweet julmust *or* svagdricka *often served in Sweden at Christmas. I like to use a chai tea blend made from a mixture of cinnamon, vanilla, cloves and cardamom that's combined with black tea leaves. Cold brewing gives tea a bigger, deeper and more complex flavour, and reduces the risk of the tea turning bitter.*

Place the tea bags and orange in a large jug or glass bowl and add 2 litres/68fl oz/8½ cups water. Stir and leave to stand in the fridge for at least 5 hours; at this point taste the tea to see if it has enough flavour – leave it to infuse for longer, if needed. Remove the tea bags once you're happy with the flavour.

GINGER BEER

PAGE 83

{makes about 2½ litres/85fl oz/10½ cups}

1 piece fresh ginger, about 5 x 3cm/2 x 1¼in, grated

125g/4½oz/heaped ½ cup granulated sugar

2–3 tbsp muscovado sugar or date syrup

150ml/5fl oz/⅔ cup lemon juice

½ tsp salt

200ml/7fl oz/generous ¾ cup Soda Culture (see below)

This recipe for ginger beer or ale, as it's sometimes referred to, is slightly time consuming to make but well worth it. It becomes naturally fizzy in time from adding a 'ginger bug', which is a type of fermented soda culture (see below) made from ginger and sugar.

Mix together the ginger, sugar, muscovado or syrup and 500ml/17fl oz/generous 2 cups water in a pan. Heat to just below 60°C/140°F, then remove from the heat. Leave to infuse for 10 minutes, then add 1.5 litres/50fl oz/ 6¼ cups water and leave to cool.

Pour the liquid into a glass jar with an airtight lid. Add the lemon juice, salt and soda culture, stir and close the lid. Leave to stand until the drink has turned fizzy – 2–5 days depending on how warm your home is and how active the soda culture is. Strain, pour into lidded bottles and leave to mature in the fridge for 10 days.

SODA CULTURE

fresh ginger

granulated sugar

Place 3 tbsp each of freshly grated peeled ginger and sugar in a large jar. Add 500ml/17fl oz/generous 2 cups water and stir with a non-metal spoon. Cover the jar with a piece of cloth or a coffee filter – a material that lets air flow through – and leave to stand at room temperature.

Add 1 tbsp sugar and 1 tbsp grated ginger, stirring the mixture every day, for 5 days or until the mixture has fermented and small bubbles have formed. The culture is now ready to use and will add fizz to your drinks.

If you want to keep the culture alive, add the same amount of water that you've removed from the jar and continue to feed it with 1 tbsp sugar and 1 tbsp grated ginger every third to fourth day.

DRINKS

COLD BREW CHAI · GINGER BEER

HOT APPLE JUICE WITH GINGER AND EARL GREY

HOT APPLE JUICE WITH GINGER AND EARL GREY

{serves 2}

500ml/7fl oz/generous 2 cups fresh apple juice

1 piece fresh ginger, about 2 x 2cm/¾ x ¾in, grated

1 tsp Earl Grey tea leaves

I pick perfect apples without bruises from my apple tree in the autumn and store them over winter – they last until late spring. The apples that have little imperfections – the ones that have fallen off the tree or are too small to store – I juice for plentiful supplies of my own fresh apple juice. I then freeze the juice in litre-sized containers and take out as and when I need it. In the winter, I like to warm the apple juice with spices, such as cinnamon, cardamom and cloves, or like here, with ginger and Earl Grey tea.

Pour the apple juice into a pan and add the ginger. Heat until just below boiling point, then remove from the heat and add the tea. Leave to infuse for a few minutes. Check the strength occasionally and when you're happy with the tea flavour, strain the drink through a mesh sieve (fine strainer). Serve immediately.

PAGE 87

{makes about
1 litre/33¾fl oz/
generous 4 cups}

140g/5oz/generous
1 cup cashew nuts

8 soft dates, pitted

500ml/17fl oz/generous
2 cups plant-based milk

½ tsp vanilla powder

1 pinch ground cinnamon

1 pinch grated nutmeg,
plus extra to serve

a little salt

50–100ml/3½–7 tbsp
rum or whisky, to taste

ice cubes

NOG

You can achieve the creamy consistency of classic egg nog from cashew nuts instead of eggs for a vegan version.

Soak the cashew nuts for at least 5 hours until softened. Strain off the soaking water and place the cashews in a blender, preferably a high-speed one. Add the dates, milk, vanilla powder, spices and salt and blend until smooth and creamy. Add the rum or whisky to taste.

Chill the nog for a few hours, then pour into glasses. Add ice and grate a little extra nutmeg over the top before serving.

GARLANDS

I decorate the house for Christmas by making garlands out of everything, such as spruce cuttings, pine cones, dried orange slices and even fresh apple slices that are left to dry hanging from the ceiling. If you eat a lot of citrus fruit in the winter, you can cut out stars or other shapes from the leftover peel, then use a needle and red thread to pierce through the peel and string them all together.

The dried orange slices almost look like old stained-glass church windows when the light shines through them. You make them simply by slicing a citrus fruit of your choice into thin, round slices (orange is the most classic choice, but lemon, lime, blood orange or even grapes are also decorative). Place the slices on a baking sheet lined with baking parchment and dry in the oven at 50°C/122°F for a couple of hours, or dry in a dehydrator. You should ideally turn the slices over a couple of times during drying so that they keep their flat shape. It's also a good idea to open the oven door from time to time to release any steam. When dried, all you have to do is thread them on to a length of pretty string to make a festive garland.

THE CHRISTMAS BUFFET

I THINK THAT SOME OF US CAN become stuck in a very traditional way of meal planning, where a meal is simply made up of meat, potatoes, veg and sauce. When the meat is removed there is an obvious empty space; a meal made from sauce, vegetables and potatoes is seen as incomplete. I feel it's because of this ingrained way of thinking that many of us find it hard to approach plant-based meals, and it's also the reason why some people wonder about protein. Yet, protein can be found in great quantities in many of our root vegetables and in grains, legumes, nuts and seeds. So, instead of focussing on what to replace meat with, the real question should be how do I make a delicious, satisfying, complete vegan meal?

For me, there are two things that make a meal feel complete and satisfying. The first is the use of different textures – it's not satisfying to eat a bowlful of smooth soup, a mushy bean burger or something deep fried with a deep-fried side. Therefore, I try to include dishes that feature a range of textures, from crispy, soft and saucy to chewy and crunchy to create a wealth of variety.

My aim with all meals is to have a contrast between the five basic tastes: salty, sweet, sour, bitter and umami. Bitter salad leaves taste good with a sweet-sour salad dressing, for instance, while sweet desserts taste better if they include a pinch of salt. If you can create balance in your dishes by basing meals on a combination of these tastes, it's easier to feel satisfied, full and content.

When you taste a meal and feel there's something missing, you can more easily identify what is lacking if you go through the basic tastes: where does the sweetness come from?; what did I use to add acidity?; is it salty enough?; and does the savoury base of umami come through? It's worth considering adding a dash of tamari or miso paste to increase both saltiness and umami, acidity can be added in the form of a few drops of cider vinegar or lemon juice, and if you're looking for sweetness in savoury food it can be found in roasted vegetables, fried onions or fruit.

Meat-free cooking can take you in two directions: there are plant-based alternatives to classic dishes, like sunflower balls instead of meatballs or Bolognese made from lentils; or go for a complete rethink and discover new dishes where the vegetables take centre stage. For me there is no conflict between these two types of cooking. I keep the traditional comfort food dishes close to heart and love to cook vegan versions of them, especially during the winter season, but I'm also just as happy to concoct completely new vegetable symphonies.

On Christmas Eve, I like to serve fairly traditional dishes and therefore mainly look to the classics, but that's a matter of taste, of course, and I know that many hunger for a Christmas celebration with colourful and not quite so heavy, brown food.

Buffets can easily become pretty time-consuming to prepare with so many different elements, but many dishes taste even better when they're prepared a few days beforehand. To avoid having to be in the kitchen all of Christmas Eve, I prepare a typical Christmas buffet featuring the dishes mentioned below.

CHRISTMAS BUFFET

VÖRTBRÖD & KAVRING (see page 33) can be baked 1–3 months in advance and stored in the freezer.

BROWN CABBAGE (see page 150) can be made 2 months in advance and frozen.

SUNFLOWER BALLS (see page 107) and/or Sticky Buffalo Cauliflower (see page 95). The balls can be made up to 2 months in advance and frozen. Fry them again after defrosting. If not freezing the balls, make up to 2 days in advance. Prepare the cauliflower on the day of serving.

BRANTEVIK PICKLES (see page 112) is made 3–4 days before serving.

BAKED PÂTÉ (see page 133) can be made 2 days in advance.

JÖNSSON'S TEMPTATION (see page 99) can be prepared and cooked 1–2 days before serving.

HUMMUS HOLIDAY BOWL (see page 104) can be made the day before serving.

PICKLED COURGETTES (see page 111) The courgettes (zucchini) can be pickled 1–2 days in advance and left in the pickling brine.

ON CHRISTMAS EVE (OR DAY OF SERVING) I like to make a double or triple batch of Vegan Mayonnaise (see page 132) and use it as the base for both the beetroot salad and the coleslaw.

COLESLAW (page 144) is prepared in conjunction with the beetroot (beet) salad and pickled courgettes.

RUSTIC ROASTED BEETROOT SALAD (see page 132) is prepared in conjunction with the coleslaw and pickled courgettes. The beetroot can be roasted the day before.

STICKY BUFFALO CAULIFLOWER

STICKY BUFFALO CAULIFLOWER

These breaded cauliflower florets are brushed with a glaze and become amazingly delicious and sweet-salty in flavour when baked. They're perfect buffet food, but can also be eaten as a snack, served with a salsa or dipping sauce.

{serves 5–7}

Cauliflower

1 garlic clove, grated

175g/6oz/1⅓ cups spelt flour or plain (all-purpose) flour, sifted

200ml/7fl oz/generous ¾ cup plant-based milk, such as soya or oat

½ tsp salt

½ tsp ground black pepper, plus extra to season

½ tsp cayenne pepper

about 125g/4½oz/3 cups panko breadcrumbs

1 whole cauliflower, leaves and stalks removed, broken into florets

fresh coriander (cilantro) and thinly sliced chilli, to garnish (optional)

Glaze

100ml/3½fl oz/generous ⅓ cup agave syrup

4 tbsp tamari

2 tbsp unhulled sesame seeds, plus extra for sprinkling

2 tsp ground ginger

Preheat the oven to 220°C/425°F/Gas 7 and line a baking sheet with baking parchment. (You may need to use two baking sheets.)

Whisk together the garlic, flour, milk, salt, pepper and cayenne in a mixing bowl to make a batter. Put the panko in a separate bowl.

Turn the florets in the batter, letting any excess drip off, then roll each floret in the panko. Place on the prepared baking sheet and roast in the oven for 20–25 minutes.

Meanwhile, mix together the ingredients for the glaze. Brush or drizzle the glaze over the cauliflower and return it to the oven for another 5–10 minutes. It's a good idea to turn the cauliflower over after a couple of minutes so that the glaze becomes evenly spread and the florets soak up any sauce that has dripped onto the paper.

Garnish the cauliflower with coriander, chilli and extra sesame seeds, if you like.

{serves 8}

Roasted vegetables

about 1.2kg/2lb 10oz root
vegetables, such as potatoes,
celeriac (celery root), parsnips
and yellow beetroot (beets),
scrubbed, peeled and cut
into bite-sized pieces

1 tbsp oil

300g/10½oz/generous 2 cups
frozen edamame (soya) beans

1 handful rocket (arugula) or
kale, tough stalks removed
and torn into shreds

Vinaigrette

1 garlic clove

2–3 handfuls fresh parsley

2–3 handfuls fresh
coriander (cilantro)

2–3 handfuls fresh mint

2 tbsp olive oil

1 tbsp lemon juice

½ yellow or green chilli

salt and black pepper

HERB-COATED
ROOT VEGETABLES

I like to use root vegetables with similar colours in a dish (here, it's white and yellow), but you can choose freely from whichever root vegetables you prefer or happen to have in the fridge. If you also make the Sticky Buffalo Cauliflower (see previous page), this is the perfect way to use up the leftover cauliflower stalks. The tangy, herby vinaigrette makes a fresh contrast to the more rich-tasting dishes on the Christmas buffet.

〜〜〜〜〜〜〜〜〜〜〜〜〜〜〜〜〜〜〜〜〜〜

Preheat the oven to 220°C/425°F/Gas 7.

Place all the root vegetables in an ovenproof dish. Add the oil and turn until everything is coated, then roast in the oven for 30–40 minutes or until tender.

Cook the edamame in boiling unsalted water for 5 minutes, drain and stir into the root vegetables once they're out of the oven.

Meanwhile, blend all the ingredients for the vinaigrette. Season with salt and pepper to taste and drizzle over the roasted root vegetables and edamame. Transfer to a serving plate and stir in the rocket or kale. (If using kale, massage the leaves first until you feel their texture softening before adding to the root vegetables.) Taste and add extra salt and pepper, if needed.

HERB-COATED ROOT VEGETABLES

CRUSHED POTATOES WITH CHILLI AND SAFFRON AIOLI

Crushed is probably my absolute favourite way to serve potatoes; they come out great every time, they are simple to prepare without fuss and, after roasting, they become both crisp and soft at the same time. Here, they are served with a chilli and saffron aioli.

{serves 5}

Potatoes

10 potatoes (you want a variety that is suitable for roasting), about 1kg/2lb 4oz total weight, skin on, scrubbed

2 tbsp olive oil

2 tsp chopped fresh rosemary, plus extra to garnish (optional)

salt and black pepper

Aioli

2 garlic cloves, peeled

100–150ml/3½–5fl oz/ generous ⅓–⅔ cup rapeseed (canola) oil

5 tbsp unsweetened soya milk

1 tsp Dijon mustard

1 pinch saffron, or to taste

1 tsp lemon juice

1 tsp sriracha or other hot chilli sauce

98
—
99

Preheat the oven to 220°C/425°F/Gas 7.

Put the potatoes on a chopping board and half-crush them one at a time, using a pestle. They should be still intact at the base so don't crush them completely.

Place the potatoes in an ovenproof dish, drizzle the olive oil over and top with a sprinkle of rosemary. Add the garlic for the aioli to the dish at the same time. Roast in the oven for 45 minutes or until the potatoes have a crisp crust and are tender inside. Season with salt and pepper.

Remove the roasted garlic from the oven and place in a blender jug with the rest of the aioli ingredients. Blend with a stick blender until a thick and creamy sauce that resembles mayonnaise. Season to taste with salt.

Garnish the potatoes with a little fresh rosemary, if you like, and serve with the aioli.

JÖNSSONS FRESTELSE / JÖNSSON'S TEMPTATION

{serves 6}

500ml/17fl oz/generous 2 cups oat cream

3 bay leaves

2 pinches ground allspice

1 pinch ground cloves

1 pinch ground ginger

1 pinch ground white pepper

1–2 tbsp mild mustard

15 potatoes (you want a variety that is suitable for mashing), about 1.2kg/2lb 10oz total weight, peeled and coarsely grated

2 large brown onions, finely chopped

2 tbsp day-old fresh breadcrumbs

3½ tbsp dairy-free spread, cut into pieces, plus extra for greasing

salt

Quite possibly my only must-have dish for a Christmas buffet is Jansson's temptation, but when I make it my vegan way it magically changes name and becomes Jönsson's temptation! I replace the flavour of the more usual spiced sprats by flavouring the oat cream with similar spices.

Preheat the oven to 200°C/400°F/Gas 6.

Gently simmer the cream, bay leaves, allspice, cloves, ginger and white pepper for 10 minutes in a pan covered with a lid. Remove the bay leaves and stir in the mustard.

Meanwhile, layer the potatoes and onions in a large, greased ovenproof dish. Salt after each layer of potato. Pour the cream mixture over, sprinkle with the breadcrumbs and finish by topping with the dairy-free spread. Bake for 1 hour or until the potatoes and onion are cooked and the top is golden.

CRUSHED POTATOES WITH CHILLI AND SAFFRON AIOLI · JÖNSSON'S TEMPTATION

GARAM MASALA BHAJIS

GARAM MASALA BHAJIS

{makes about 12 bhajis}

4 brown or red onions,
coarsely grated

1 tsp salt

2 garlic cloves, chopped

1 green chilli, finely chopped

125g/4½oz/1 cup gram
(chickpea) flour

1 tsp ground cinnamon

½ tsp ground turmeric

½ tsp ground cumin

1 pinch crushed
cardamom seeds

1 pinch ground cloves

vegetable oil, for frying

In my last book Goodness Green *I also included a recipe for bhajis – although flavoured differently and served as burgers – so I contemplated for a long time whether to include a recipe in this book. However, since bhajis are quick to make and are a dish that I often serve as part of a buffet, I really wanted to include them in this book. Here, I have flavoured the bhajis, or onion fritters, with garam masala spices to give them a taste of Christmas.*

Place the onions in a mixing bowl, add the salt and knead until the onions soften and start to release liquid. Leave to stand for a few minutes.

Add the garlic and chilli to the bowl with the gram flour, cinnamon, turmeric, cumin, cardamom, cloves and 2 tablespoons water and mix together well. Shape the mixture into 12 bhajis.

Heat a generous amount of oil in a large frying pan (skillet) over a medium heat. Cook the bhajis in batches for 3–4 minutes, turning once, until golden brown all over. Drain on kitchen paper before serving.

PAGE 105

{makes about
1kg/2lb 4oz}

4 medium raw beetroot
(beets), scrubbed and
cut into wedges

1 garlic clove, skin on
and cut in half

100ml/3½fl oz/generous
⅓ cup olive oil, plus
extra for drizzling

4 x 400g/14oz cans cooked
chickpeas (garbanzos), drained

juice of 1 lemon

1 tsp sesame oil

1–2 tsp dried thyme

salt and black pepper

Topping

olives, chioggia beetroot
(beets), thyme, rosemary,
unhulled white and
black sesame seeds

HUMMUS HOLIDAY BOWL

*No veggie feast is complete without a bucketful of hummus!
This is quite an enormous batch, but I like to serve hummus in
a really big bowl with seasonal vegetables topping it all off. This
time of year, it's particularly perfect to serve loads of roasted root
vegetables, carrot sticks and raw broccoli and cauliflower florets
with the hummus for a true finger food experience.*

*The wonderful red colour that looks so good on the Christmas
table comes from roasted beetroot (beets) which, as well as the
roasted garlic and herbs, add flavour to the hummus.*

~~~~~~

Preheat the oven to 220°C/425°F/Gas 7.

Place the beetroot in an ovenproof dish with the
garlic. Drizzle a little olive oil over the top and roast for
30 minutes or until the beetroot have softened. Leave to
cool slightly, then squeeze the garlic out of its skin.

Put all the ingredients in a blender, preferably a high-
speed one, or use a stick blender. If you use a blender
with a bowl you may need to do this in two batches, since
this is a real mega batch. Add 200ml/7fl oz/generous
¾ cup water and blend until smooth and creamy. Season
to taste with salt and pepper.

The hummus in the picture is topped with olives,
thinly sliced chioggia beetroot, thyme, rosemary and
unhulled white and black sesame seeds.

HUMMUS HOLIDAY BOWL

SUNFLOWER BALLS

SUNFLOWER BALLS

2 tbsp psyllium husk

140g/5oz/1 cup
sunflower seeds

1 large brown onion, chopped

30g/1oz/¾ cup day-old
fresh breadcrumbs

1 tbsp tamari

1 tsp salt

½ tsp white pepper

1 pinch ground allspice

oil, for frying

It may have been several years since I last ate meat, but if I try to remember the flavour of meatballs, it's actually just like how these sunflower balls taste. It was also the first dish on the family's combined Christmas and Easter buffet that was wholly replaced with a vegan version. I love them as they are easy to make and fantastic, whether served with Jönsson's Temptation (see page 99) at the Christmas buffet or with the classic boiled potatoes and gravy!

Mix together the psyllium husk and 150ml/5fl oz/⅔ cup water and leave to swell for 10 minutes while you prepare the sunflower seeds and onion.

Blitz the sunflower seeds into a flour in a food processor or blender. Add the onion and the remaining ingredients and quickly blend together into a firm mixture. You could also finely chop the onion by hand and stir it into the rest of the ingredients in a bowl.

Roll the mixture into even-sized balls, about 25 in total.

Heat a generous amount of oil in a large frying pan (skillet) over a medium heat. Cook the balls in batches for 3–4 minutes, turning once, until nicely coloured all the way round. Drain on kitchen paper before serving.

RADICCHIO CANAPÉS WITH CASHEW CHEESE SALAD

{makes about 20}

Cashew cheese

210g/7½oz/scant
2 cups cashew nuts

2 probiotic capsules

½ tbsp lemon juice

1 tbsp cider vinegar

1 heaped tbsp coconut oil

2 tsp nutritional yeast flakes

Mushroom mixture

1 tbsp olive oil

15g/½oz chestnut (cremini)
mushrooms, quartered

1 tsp dried thyme

1 small red onion, chopped

4 good handfuls fresh
parsley, chopped

salt and black pepper

Salad and garnishes

70g/2½oz/½ cup
sunflower seeds

2–3 whole radicchio
lettuces, leaves separated

cress

pomegranate seeds

These beautiful canapés are served in long radicchio leaves. I think the wonderful red colour is perfect for Christmas, but if you can't get hold of radicchio you can replace it with chicory (endive). Chicory also comes in a red variety, which would be just as nice.

The probiotics used in the cashew cheese can be found at the pharmacy, in health food stores or supermarkets and they help to firm up the cheese over time. Exclude the nutritional yeast or use less of it if you want to make a sweeter cheese, such as cashew cheese with raisins and pistachios, which is delicious on ginger snaps. If you don't want to make your own cashew cheese, buy plant-based quark or fraîche instead and flavour it with nutritional yeast, salt and black pepper, or opt for a sweet alternative.

~~~~~~

To make the cheese, soak the cashews in cold water for at least 5 hours. Strain off the soaking water, then place the nuts and the rest of the ingredients for the cashew cheese in a high-speed blender. Add 2 tablespoons water and blend until smooth. Spoon into a lidded container and leave in the fridge for 24 hours or longer to mature.

To prepare the mushroom mixture, heat the oil in a frying pan (skillet) over a medium heat. Add the mushrooms and sauté until they've coloured nicely. Stir in the thyme towards the end, then leave to cool.

Mix together the cashew cheese, mushrooms, onion and parsley. Season to taste with salt and pepper.

Toast the sunflower seeds in a large, dry frying pan (skillet) until they've coloured nicely and start to pop, then leave to cool. Arrange the radicchio leaves on a large serving plate. Add a dollop of the cashew mixture onto each salad leaf, and garnish with cress, sunflower seeds and pomegranate seeds.

RADICCHIO CANAPÉS WITH CASHEW CHEESE SALAD

PICKLED COURGETTES

{serves 4–6}

90g/3¼oz/scant ½ cup granulated sugar

1½ tbsp distilled vinegar (24%)

½ tsp salt

1 courgette (zucchini), peeled and cut into bite-sized chunks

Mayonnaise

150ml/5fl oz/⅔ cup rapeseed (canola) oil

5 tbsp unsweetened soya milk

1 tsp Dijon or 1 tbsp Skånsk mustard

1 tsp lemon juice

salt

I think that the acidity of pickles goes very well with the rich Christmas dishes that can be found on the Christmas buffet. One of my favourites is pickled courgettes (zucchini), which I flavour with a variety of mayonnaise dressings.

Courgettes can actually be prepared and pickled around August to September when they're in season, but you could choose imported courgettes instead around Christmas. If you put the lid on while the liquid is still hot, the courgettes are preserved in the same way as pickled cucumbers.

To make a brine, mix together the sugar, vinegar and salt with 200ml/7fl oz/generous ¾ cup water in a pan. Bring to the boil and add the courgette. Simmer for a couple of minutes, then remove from the heat. Leave the courgette to cool in the brine until you mix it into one of the mayonnaise dressings. You can, however, remove the courgette from the hot brine if it starts to get too soft, and then put it back once the brine has cooled.

Blend together all the ingredients for the mayonnaise. Choose two dressings from those listed below. Stir one dressing into half of the mayonnaise in a bowl, then the other dressing into the remaining mayonnaise in a separate bowl – or make a double batch of one dressing. Season with salt. Remove the courgette from the brine and divide it between each one and stir to combine.

HORSERADISH

1 tbsp grated fresh horseradish

½ tsp golden syrup (light corn syrup) or agave syrup

MUSTARD

2 tsp Dijon mustard or 2 tbsp Skånsk mustard

5 tbsp chopped dill, fresh or frozen

½ tsp golden syrup (light corn syrup) or agave syrup

ARCHIPELAGO

3 tbsp seaweed caviar

½ red onion, chopped

3 good handfuls chopped dill, fresh or frozen

½ tsp golden syrup (light corn syrup) or agave syrup

CURRY

1 tsp curry powder of choice

1 apple, peeled, cored and chopped or sliced

½ tsp golden syrup (light corn syrup) or agave syrup

PAGE 113

BRANTEVIK PICKLES

{makes 1 jar}

Brantevik pickles, which traditionally come from the little fishing village of Brantevik in Österlen, make an appearance on the buffet table both at Christmas and Easter at my place. Yet my version is made from mushrooms, rather than the more usual herrings. I find that mushrooms have a lovely texture and consistency for pickling.

Brine

1 tsp salt

2 tbsp distilled vinegar (24%)

Mushrooms and flavourings

250g/9oz/3¾ cups mushrooms, such as shiitake or portobello, cut into pieces

1 red onion, finely chopped

1 brown onion, finely chopped

3 bay leaves, torn

15 white peppercorns, crushed

15 whole allspice, crushed

1 tsp coarsely ground black pepper

1 tsp finely grated lemon zest

70g/2½oz/⅓ cup granulated sugar

6 large handfuls chopped dill, fresh or frozen

To make a brine, place the salt and vinegar in a small pan with 300ml/10½fl oz/generous 1¼ cups water. Bring to the boil and add the mushrooms. Remove from the heat and leave the mushrooms to cool in the brine.

Place the onions, bay, spices, lemon zest, sugar and dill in a glass jar and stir. Fish out the mushrooms with a slotted spoon, add them to the jar and stir so that the mushrooms are mixed in with the other ingredients. Put on a lid and leave the pickle to stand in a cool place for 3 days. Store the jar in the fridge when opened.

CREAMED KALE IN POTATO PASTRY

CREAMED KALE IN POTATO PASTRY

This tart has a gluten-free pastry case made with boiled potatoes and rice flour, and is therefore perfect for people who are intolerant to gluten. Or anyone who has boiled potatoes that need using up! The tart is a nod to the traditional festive creamed kale (långkål) *from Halland County in west Sweden and is therefore just right for the Christmas buffet.*

{serves 6}

Pastry

350g/12oz boiled and peeled potatoes, grated

70g/2½oz/generous ½ cup rice flour

5 tbsp rapeseed (canola) or coconut oil, plus extra for greasing

Filling

olive oil

150g/5½oz kale, tough stalks discarded, leaves shredded

½ leek, thinly sliced

1 shallot, finely chopped

1 garlic clove, thinly sliced

½ chilli, finely chopped

250ml/9fl oz/generous 1 cup oat cream

1 tsp Dijon mustard or 1 tbsp Skånsk mustard

1 tsp dried thyme

1 pinch grated nutmeg

salt and black pepper

Garnishes

pea shoots

toasted flaked almonds

Preheat the oven to 200°C/400°F/Gas 6. Mix the potatoes with the rice flour and oil to form a firm dough. Press the dough out in a greased tart tin (pan). Line with baking parchment and beans and bake blind for 10 minutes or until light golden.

Meanwhile, make the filling. Heat a little olive oil in a frying pan (skillet) and sauté the kale, leek, shallot, garlic and chilli until the leek has softened and turned shiny. Add the oat cream and season with mustard, thyme and nutmeg. Add salt and pepper, to taste.

Remove the paper and beans from the pastry case. Spoon in the filling and smooth the top, then bake the tart for 20 minutes until slightly firm and the pastry is cooked through.

Garnish with pea shoots and almonds before serving.

MUSTARD SEED POTATO SALAD WITH CRESS AND POMEGRANATE

{serves 6–8}

Potatoes

1kg/2lb 4oz potatoes with skin on, scrubbed and cut into bite-sized pieces

1 tbsp oil

Mayonnaise

2 garlic cloves, peeled

5 tbsp unsweetened soya milk

150ml/5fl oz/⅔ cup rapeseed (canola) oil

1 tsp Dijon mustard or 1 tbsp Skånsk mustard

½ tbsp lemon juice

3 pinches salt

black pepper

Garnishes

1 tbsp mustard seeds

3 sprigs of dill, coarsely chopped

4 tbsp pomegranate seeds

cress

Certain foods, when roasted until crisp and golden, simply become a little bit more delicious. So that's exactly what I've decided to do with the potatoes in this potato salad, which is fantastic with dill, toasted mustard seeds, peppery cress and crunchy, sweet pomegranate seeds. It's best when eaten slightly warm or at room temperature, but can also be served straight from the fridge.

Preheat the oven to 220°C/425°F/Gas 7.

Place the potatoes in an ovenproof dish and toss them in the oil. At the same time, add the garlic for the mayonnaise. Roast for 45 minutes, or until the potatoes are tender and coloured nicely. Take out and leave them to cool slightly.

Blend together the ingredients for the mayonnaise with the roasted garlic until smooth and creamy.

Toast the mustard seeds over a low heat in a dry frying pan (skillet) for 1 minute or until they smell fragrant.

Mix together the potatoes and the mayonnaise, check the flavours and add more seasoning, if needed. Spoon onto a serving plate and top with the dill, pomegranate seeds, cress and toasted mustard seeds.

MUSTARD SEED POTATO SALAD WITH CRESS AND POMEGRANATE

COLESLAW SOMBRE

COLESLAW SOMBRE

📷

PAGE 118

{serves 6–8}

Salad

500g/1lb 2oz cabbage, preferably a mix of red and white, shredded

2–3 handfuls mung bean sprouts

2–3 handfuls dried cranberries, goji berries or raisins

3 tbsp unhulled sesame seeds, plus extra to garnish (I used a mixture of black and white)

¼ nori sheet, shredded (optional)

Dressing

2 small garlic cloves, peeled

2 tbsp tahini

3 tbsp olive oil

1½ tbsp lemon juice

salt and black pepper

This slaw is a great side dish for the Christmas buffet as it brings a crisp freshness to the table, while the dried cranberries make an appealing sweet and chewy contrast. I also like the fantastic sombre colours of purple, pink and black – it almost looks like a rain-laden, windswept December day!

This would make a great alternative to your regular type of creamy coleslaw.

~~~~~~~~~~~~~~~~~~~~~~~~~~~~~~~~

Place the cabbage in a bowl with the mung bean sprouts, cranberries and sesame seeds.

Blend together the ingredients for the dressing with 3 tablespoons water. Drizzle it over the salad and top with a few extra pinches of sesame seeds and the nori, if you like.

WHOLE ROASTED ONIONS

📷

PAGE 120

{serves 8}

500g/1lb 2oz baby onions, peeled

vegetable oil, for drizzling

thyme and sage sprigs

salt and black pepper

Roasted onions work as a side to most dishes. Besides, any leftover roasted onions make the perfect alternative to raw onion.

~~~~~~~~~~~~~~~~~~~~~~~~~~~~~~~~

Preheat the oven to 150°C/300°F/Gas 2.

Place the onions in an ovenproof dish. Drizzle over a little oil and turn until they are coated, then top with the thyme and sage. Roast for 1 hour, or until the onions have softened. Sprinkle with salt and pepper, to taste.

WHOLE ROASTED ONIONS

Porridge is a Christmas classic for me and here I've given varieties for any occasion and to suit every taste: classic rice porridge; a healthy and protein-rich, cinnamon-infused buckwheat porridge; and a raw oat and seed porridge, which I think is particularly great for breakfast.

📷

PAGE 124

{serves 4–6}

250g/9oz/1⅔ cups whole hulled buckwheat

500–700ml/17–23fl oz/ generous 2–3 cups oat milk

3 cinnamon sticks

1 tsp vanilla powder or extract

3 tbsp agave syrup, or to taste

To serve

2 x 400g/14oz cans coconut milk

apple sauce (see below), strawberry compote or jam of choice

persimmon

ground cinnamon

orange zest is obligatory!

Apple sauce

3 apples, cored

1 piece fresh ginger, about 3cm/1¼in or to taste, peeled and finely grated

finely grated zest of 1 lemon

CINNAMON-INFUSED BUCKWHEAT PORRIDGE

Soak the buckwheat overnight or for at least 5 hours. Transfer the buckwheat to a mesh sieve (fine strainer) and rinse it under cold running water until the gel coating is removed. Place the buckwheat in a pan and cover with water, bring to the boil and simmer for a few minutes. Strain off the liquid and quickly rinse the buckwheat again. Return it to the pan, add the oat milk and the rest of the ingredients and simmer for 15 minutes, stirring occasionally, until cooked. Serve hot, warm or cold.

BUCKWHEAT À LA MALTA

Place the coconut milk in the fridge for a couple of hours. Open the cans and scoop out the firm coconut cream on the top. (The remaining coconut water can be added to smoothies.) Whisk the coconut milk until fluffy and stir it into the cold buckwheat porridge. Serve the buckwheat porridge with strawberry compote/jam, persimmon, cinnamon and orange zest, for example.

APPLE SAUCE

Blend all the ingredients with 3–4 tablespoons water and serve with the buckwheat porridge and other toppings of your choice.

CLASSIC RICE PORRIDGE

〜〜〜〜〜〜〜〜〜〜〜〜〜〜

{serves 4–6}

185g/6½oz/1 cup pudding rice

1–2 cinnamon sticks

600ml/21fl oz/2½ cups
plant milk of your choice

2 pinches vanilla powder

1 tbsp agave syrup or
other sweetener

Put the pudding rice and cinnamon sticks in a pan with 500ml/17fl oz/generous 2 cups water. Bring to the boil, then turn down the heat and simmer on a low heat for 10 minutes, stirring occasionally. Add the plant milk and simmer for another 30 minutes, stirring occasionally, or until the rice is cooked. Add the vanilla powder and agave syrup, to taste. It's great served with lingonberry jam (see jam tip below), ground cinnamon and finely grated orange zest.

RAW OAT AND SEED PORRIDGE

〜〜〜〜〜〜〜〜〜〜〜〜〜〜

{serves 1}

1 banana, mashed

50g/1¾oz/heaped ½ cup
rolled porridge oats

1 tbsp each of unhulled sesame
seeds, linseeds, sunflower
seeds and chia seeds

150ml/5fl oz/⅔ cup plant milk,
or to required consistency

To serve, choose from:

diced blood orange, pomegranate seeds, frozen sea buckthorn, berries and lingonberries, coconut flakes, cranberry powder, cacao nibs, hulled hemp seeds, dried mulberries, strawberry jam and finely grated orange zest

Mix the banana in a bowl with the oats, seeds and plant milk, then leave the oats to swell for at least 20–30 minutes, preferably 1 hour. The porridge can also be prepared the night before (if so, leave it to stand in the fridge overnight). If the consistency is too thick, add a bit more milk and if it looks too runny you can leave it to swell for a bit longer. Serve the porridge with your choice of toppings.

JAM TIP

Instead of buying jam or making it with jam sugar, pectin or other thickening agents, I freeze strawberries during the summer, then when I need jam I boil the strawberries in a tiny, tiny amount of water and sweeten it with agave syrup. The strawberries are left to cool, then I add 1 tablespoon chia seeds, which thicken the jam. The seeds are left to do their work for a couple of hours before serving.

CINNAMON-INFUSED BUCKWHEAT PORRIDGE · BUCKWHEAT À LA MALTA

· CLASSIC RICE PORRIDGE · RAW OAT AND SEED PORRIDGE

WREATHS

It is easy to make an attractive festive wreath. To make a thin wreath, simply shape a piece of sturdy wire into a circle, then attach greens, such as spruce sprigs, box or ivy, by winding black thread around the sprigs and wire. Add a new sprig before the old one is fully tied down so that they overlap nicely. If you prefer a bushy wreath, simply leave the tip of the sprig unattached so that it protrudes a little.

If you are looking for a thicker wreath, such as a door wreath, it is a good idea to use a frame. The absolute easiest way is, of course, to buy a ready-made frame, but you can also make one from materials such as straw, dried grass or bendy twigs like birch, which are things that you can easily find outdoors in nature or in your garden.

Arrange your chosen material into a length, making sure it overlaps, and tie together with several rounds of thread, then shape it into a circle and secure the two ends. For extra stability, you can include a thick wire running through the middle of the frame, which will make shaping the wreath into a circle easier.

Now it's time to attach your greens around the frame. For this, tie down sprigs using a thin wire or dark thread. Arrange the sprigs so that they overlap; I like to leave the tips of my sprigs sticking out – and to do this simply leave the tip of the sprig unattached and wind the thread underneath it instead, which will allow you to attach the next sprig properly.

In the wreath pictured opposite, once the whole wreath was dressed in spruce, I attached a few sprigs of ivy to create a contrast between the needles and leaves. Mature ivy produces very decorative seed balls that I thought looked extra pretty, almost like a mini bouquet.

LEFTOVERS

CHRISTMAS DAY is over, the table has been cleared and you may find yourself with leftovers waiting to be used up. In this chapter, I explore what can be created from leftover ingredients and surplus cooked and uncooked food. Several of the following dishes also make use of component recipes that could be included in the Christmas buffet table, such as: the brown cabbage that is used for the cabbage bake; the beetroot (beet) salad for the sunflower ball sandwich; the coleslaw, which is served with the pulled jackfruit; or the winter rolls, for that matter, either as they are prepared here as rolls, or as a salad without the rice paper wrappers.

This is what is so darn lovely about buffet or finger foods; they can often be easily rejigged and transformed into delicious new dishes. It is a way of eating that I feel we could try to apply to everyday cooking as well, since it encourages us to be creative with our leftovers and the foods that we buy. Perhaps it is also a way of seeing the plant-based kitchen from a different perspective, enabling us to break away from the classic way of putting together a meal. I believe this way of thinking enables us to enjoy varied and colourful dinners with food that everyone likes, both for weekdays and feasts.

SUET CUPS FOR WINTER GARDEN BIRDS

500g/1lb 2oz coconut oil (you can use a refined one, if you like)

100ml/3½fl oz/generous ⅓ cup rapeseed (canola) oil

700g/1lb 9oz/5 cups mixed wild bird seed

Melt the coconut oil in a pan and stir in the rapeseed oil and seeds. Scoop the mixture into old cups (or other vessels such as milk bottles or plastic containers). To make sure the birds can sit and enjoy picking their seeds, I insert a stick into each cup. Leave the fat to set. Tie string or a ribbon around the cup's handle and hang it up in a tree or at a bird feeding station. For my chickens, I make seed cups without inserting sticks.

If you have a garden, you can start planning for the next growing season in the winter. If you sow sunflowers, it's possible to harvest your own sunflower seeds come autumn and then use home-grown seeds for the winter bird treats. You can, of course, also use the seeds for sprouting chlorophyll-packed sunflower sprouts for mixing into salads or topping your breakfast bread.

SMØRREBRØD / DANISH OPEN SANDWICHES 📷 PAGE 134

I love sandwiches! And with a bit of Danish finesse even a boring old sandwich can be transformed into a delicacy. Here are recipes for two variations of sunflower ball sandwiches, as well as a baked pâté sandwich and a homemade cashew mozzarella – all served on dark rye bread. It's like a mini Christmas buffet in a smörgåsbord format!

SUNFLOWER BALL SANDWICH X 2

1 recipe quantity Sunflower Balls (see page 107)

dark rye bread, to serve

Rustic roasted beetroot salad

4 beetroot (beets), about 300g/10½oz, peeled and cut into wedges

100ml/3½fl oz/generous ⅓ cup neutral-tasting oil

50g/1¾oz/heaped ⅓ cup chopped pickled beetroot (beets)

salt and black pepper

Vegan mayonnaise

3½ tbsp unsweetened soya milk

½ tsp Dijon mustard or ½ tbsp Skånsk mustard

½ tsp lemon juice

Preheat the oven to 220°C /425°F/Gas 7. Place the beetroot in an ovenproof dish and coat it in a little of the oil. Roast for 30 minutes or until tender. Leave to cool.

Blend the remaining oil, soya milk, mustard and lemon juice into a thick mayonnaise, then stir in the roasted and pickled beetroots. Season to taste.

Tartare sauce

100ml/3½fl oz/generous ⅓ cup neutral-tasting oil

3½ tbsp unsweetened soya milk

½ tsp Dijon mustard or ½ tbsp Skånsk mustard

½ tsp lemon juice

4–5 tbsp chopped pickles or gherkins

ground turmeric, for colour

salt and black pepper

Blend the oil, milk, mustard and lemon into a thick mayonnaise. Stir in the pickles and turmeric to add colour. Season.

Caramelized onions

1 tbsp rapeseed (canola) oil

3 large brown onions, thinly sliced

salt and black pepper

Heat the oil in a frying pan (skillet), add the onions and fry for 15–20 minutes over a medium–low heat until golden and caramelized. Season to taste.

To assemble the two types of open sandwiches: serve the sunflower balls with the beetroot mayonnaise, or with the tartare sauce and caramelized onions.

BAKED PÂTÉ SANDWICH

1 small brown onion, chopped

50g/1¾oz/heaped ½ cup rolled porridge oats

15g/½oz/⅓ cup fresh day-old breadcrumbs

200ml/7fl oz/generous ¾ cup oat milk

2 tbsp rapeseed (canola) oil

15–20g/½—⅔oz cup fresh yeast (or about 7.5–10g/¼–⅓ oz dried)

½ tbsp stock powder

½ tbsp tamari

½ tsp dried marjoram

2 pinches ground white pepper

1 pinch ground allspice

salt

dark rye bread, to serve

Deep-fried leek roots (optional)

roots from fresh leeks, washed thoroughly and drained on kitchen paper

oil, for deep frying

Preheat the oven to 170°C /325°F/Gas 3. Mix all the ingredients for the pâté together in a bowl and leave to stand for a few minutes to allow the mixture to swell. Blend using a stick blender until the onion and oats are smooth. Spoon the mixture into a small greased ovenproof dish and bake for 1 hour.

Pour enough oil in a pan to deep fry the leek roots. Heat to 160°C/320°F. Add the leek roots and cook briefly until nicely coloured. Drain well.

To serve, top rye bread with the pâté and the leeks. (You could also add pickled cucumber and roasted onion.)

CASHEW MOZZARELLA AND PESTO SANDWICH

Cashew mozzarella

100g/3½oz/¾ cup cashew nuts

1 tbsp psyllium husk

1 tsp lemon juice

salt

Kale pesto

3 large kale leaves, tough stalks removed, leaves shredded

½ garlic clove, peeled

3 tbsp olive oil

3 tbsp nuts (I use 50:50 pine nuts and cashew nuts or seeds)

1 tbsp nutritional yeast flakes

1 tsp lemon juice

black pepper

dark rye bread, to serve

Soak the cashew nuts for at least 5 hours in cold water. Mix the psyllium husk with 150ml/5fl oz/⅔ cup water and leave to swell for 2 hours.

Drain the cashew nuts. Place all the ingredients for the cashew mozzarella in a high-speed blender and blend to a thick curd. Tip into a container and leave to stand in the fridge for 2 hours. Tear into pieces or cut into slices.

To make the kale pesto, blend all the ingredients together until almost smooth. Season to taste.

To serve, top rye bread with the cashew mozzarella and kale pesto.

SMØRREBRØD / DANISH OPEN SANDWICHES

SUN-YELLOW ENERGY SOUP

SUN-YELLOW ENERGY SOUP

Soup

1 large brown onion, chopped

oil of your choice

1–2 cinnamon sticks,
crushed into small pieces

900g/2lb sweet potatoes
or pumpkin, peeled
and cut into cubes

1 red chilli, chopped

5 dried lime leaves or
1 lemongrass stick

400g/14oz can coconut milk

salt and black pepper

To serve (optional)

sprouts, shoots, shredded
cabbage, cress or raw
cauliflower florets

toasted or untoasted
seeds or nuts

oat fraîche

As written previously in this book, I feel it's more important than ever to eat colourful food when the time of year is at its greyest and darkest. This sun-yellow soup shines with energy and is quick to make. When serving smooth blended soups, I think you can embrace the same way of thinking as when you're making smoothie bowls, that is to top them with anything you've got kicking about (see my suggestions below).

Sauté the onion in a little oil in a large pan until it has softened and starts to colour. Season with salt and pepper. Add the cinnamon sticks and fry with the onion for another couple of minutes.

Add the sweet potatoes or pumpkin, chilli and lime leaves or lemongrass to the pan, stir, and sauté for a little longer.

Add 800ml/27fl oz/3½ cups water and the coconut milk. Bring almost to the boil, then turn the heat down and simmer for 15 minutes or until the sweet potatoes have softened. Remove and discard the lime leaves or lemongrass and blend the soup until smooth. (You could set a few chunks of sweet potato to one side to serve them whole in the soup.) Add salt and pepper to taste and top with your toppings of choice.

The soup in the picture is served with cress, sunflower seeds, black sesame seeds and oat fraîche.

{makes 5}

Bread

10g/⅓oz fresh yeast (or about 5g/⅛oz dried)

1 tsp salt

380g/13½oz/scant 3 cups spelt flour, sifted, plus extra for dusting

Filling

1 leek (use both the white and green parts), rinsed well and sliced

2 tbsp olive oil

1 garlic clove, chopped

½ green chilli, chopped

3–4 cold boiled and peeled potatoes, about 350g/12oz total weight

4 good handfuls fresh coriander (cilantro) or parsley, chopped

salt and black pepper

BOLANI

These calzone-type bread parcels are traditionally from Afghanistan, where they are usually made with a filling of boiled potato and fried onion or leek. That said, you can, of course, throw in any leftovers that you've got to hand – think how nice it would be to add a dollop of lentil mince leftover from a taco night!

Crumble the yeast into a bowl, add 250ml/9fl oz/ generous 1 cup lukewarm water and stir until the yeast has dissolved. Add the salt and flour and work together into a smooth dough. Place in a bowl and leave to rise for 1 hour, covered with a cloth.

To make the filling, fry the leek in three-quarters of the oil until softened. Add the garlic and chilli and sauté briefly. Mash the potatoes using a fork and add to the leeks with the herbs. Add salt and pepper, to taste.

Divide the dough into 5 pieces. Roll each piece out on a lightly floured work surface to a thin round similar to a small pizza base. Place a dollop of the filling in one half of the dough, then fold the other half over. Pinch the edges together to seal in the filling. Repeat to make 5 bolani in total.

Heat a little of the remaining oil in a frying pan (skillet), add 2–3 bolani, flatten them slightly using a spatula and cook over a medium heat for a couple of minutes on each side. Repeat with the remaining oil and bolani. They are nice served warm with a dipping sauce made from oat fraîche.

📷

PAGE 141

{makes 12}

Rolls

¼ head red cabbage, finely shredded

1 small whole broccoli head, thinly sliced

12 rice paper wrappers

2 carrots, cut into thin sticks

1 handful pea shoots

2–3 handfuls fresh coriander (cilantro), leaves and stalks separated (use the stalks in the dressing)

black and white sesame seeds and cress, to garnish

Dressing

5 soft dates, pitted

1 garlic clove, peeled

1 piece fresh ginger, about 3 x 3cm/1¼in, peeled and roughly chopped

100ml/3½fl oz/generous ⅓ cup olive oil

3½ tbsp lemon juice

5 sun-dried tomatoes

2 tbsp peanut butter

2 tbsp cider vinegar

½ chilli, deseeded

salt

RAW WINTER ROLLS

These raw winter rolls are perfect for a packed lunch or picnic for winter days out. Packed with umami flavour, the dressing really makes them something special. It contains sun-dried tomatoes and peanut butter, which almost makes the shredded vegetables seem cooked, even though they are actually raw. The dressing is also sweet from the dates, sour from the lemon juice and cider vinegar, hot from the chilli and contains saltiness – a perfect mix of the five basic tastes. This is a trick that I like to use when preparing raw food; a breadth of flavour means that we become more satisfied and content after eating.

Place the red cabbage and broccoli in a bowl.

Blend together all the ingredients for the dressing, including the coriander stalks, until smooth. Add salt to taste. Pour the dressing over the cabbage and broccoli and turn until combined.

Soak a rice paper sheet in water, take it out after a minute or so, once it feels pliable, and place on a work surface. Wipe off any excess water with your hand. Place a dollop of cabbage salad just below the middle of the sheet, add a few carrot sticks, pea shoots and coriander leaves. Fold the sides of the rice paper over the filling and roll up, starting from the bottom, and press to seal the top. Repeat with the wrappers and filling.

RAW WINTER ROLLS

FALSE FISH DINNER

FALSE FISH DINNER

{serves 4}

'Fish'

185g/6½oz/1 cup pudding rice or other short grain rice

2 small brown onions, finely chopped

400g/14oz can white beans, drained

about 100g/3½oz/2 cups panko breadcrumbs

rapeseed oil, for frying

salt and ground white pepper

To serve

boiled green peas

boiled or mashed potato

cold dill sauce (made from oat fraîche, vegan mayonnaise, lemon juice and chopped fresh dill)

lemon wedges

If you make your own rice porridge or pudding over Christmas, you may have some uncooked pudding rice left over. This particularly sticky rice makes a surprisingly good alternative to minced fish, especially when coated in panko and fried until golden. My dad was occasionally served false fish made from semolina in his youth, but I think that pudding rice makes a much better fish alternative.

Something to keep in mind when it comes to classic comfort food is to make an effort with the sides. Often it's actually the sides that contribute to that reassuring nostalgic feeling. So don't hold back on the mash or boiled potatoes, peas and dill sauce – these are the dishes that put the 'comfort' in 'comfort food'!

Put the rice in a pan and pour in 400ml/13½fl oz/scant 1¾ cups water. Bring to the boil, then turn the heat to low, cover with a lid, and simmer until the rice is tender and all the water has been absorbed. Add the onions and beans. Blend the mixture until the beans and onion are finely chopped and mixed in with the rice – the mixture should be like a coarse mince or paste. Add salt and pepper, to taste, and leave to cool completely.

Shape the rice mixture into 4 fillets. Pour the panko into a bowl, add a splash of water and stir. Coat the fillets in the panko, pressing them down slightly so the crumbs stick all over.

Heat enough oil to generously coat a large frying pan (skillet) over a medium heat. Fry the fillets for 3–5 minutes on each side until golden. Serve the fillets with peas, boiled or mashed potato, dill sauce and lemon wedges on the side.

🖾

PAGE 146

{serves 6}

Jackfruit

4 brown onions, thinly sliced

rapeseed (canola) oil

4 garlic cloves, finely chopped

1 chilli, finely chopped

2 x 585g/1lb 4oz cans
jackfruit in brine, drained

1 tsp chilli powder

2 x 400g/14oz cans
chopped tomatoes

3 tbsp tamari

salt and black pepper

Coleslaw

200g/7oz white
cabbage, shredded

2 carrots, shredded

1 red onion, shredded

100ml/3½fl oz/generous
⅓ cup neutral-tasting oil

3½ tbsp unsweetened
soya milk

1 tsp Dijon mustard or
1 tbsp Skånsk mustard

½ tbsp lemon juice

200ml/7fl oz/generous
¾ cup oat fraîche

To serve

tortilla wraps

fresh coriander
(cilantro) leaves

finely sliced chilli (optional)

lemon wedges

PULLED JACKFRUIT

For my Christmas buffet I always include a big bowl of coleslaw, one of winter's many lovely salads. If I have any left over, I like to rustle up a pot of pulled jackfruit in the days after Christmas to serve with the coleslaw. Serve in tortillas, wraps or sourdough buns and top with plenty of fresh coriander (cilantro). The Coleslaw Sombre (see page 119) is also a great alternative to the rich and creamy version here.

You will find canned jackfruit in Asian food stores and some supermarkets and it comes in both brine and syrup. For this recipe, it's the version in brine that you need.

〜〜〜〜〜〜〜〜〜〜〜〜〜〜〜〜〜〜

Fry the onions in rapeseed oil over a medium heat until they have softened and turned golden. Season with salt and pepper, to taste. Add the garlic, chilli and jackfruit and sauté for a couple of minutes, then add the chilli powder. Sauté for another couple of minutes, then add the chopped tomatoes and tamari and leave to simmer, part-covered with a lid, for 1 hour until reduced and thickened. Crush the jackfruit pieces with the back of a wooden spoon, check the flavouring and add more seasoning if needed.

To make the coleslaw, put the cabbage, carrots and onion in a large bowl. Blend the oil, soya milk, mustard and lemon juice to form a thick mayonnaise. Mix the oat fraîche with the mayonnaise and add to the vegetables, then turn until mixed together. Season with salt and pepper, to taste.

To serve, place the jackfruit mixture in tortilla wraps and top with coleslaw, coriander leaves and chilli, if using. Serve with lemon wedges for squeezing over.

JERUSALEM ARTICHOKE PIZZAS

Jerusalem artichokes are in season at this time of the year and I'm fortunate to grow them in my garden. I love the feeling of digging the tubers up from the cold, sleeping winter soil, but you can, of course, also buy them. I top these pizzas with a purée made from Jerusalem artichokes and white beans, and a few kale leaves, sliced red onion and fresh sage leaves.

{makes 3–4}

Base

20g/⅔oz fresh yeast (or about 10g/⅓oz dried)

1 tbsp olive oil

625g/1lb 6oz/heaped 4½ cups plain (all-purpose) flour, plus extra for dusting

½ tbsp salt

Purée

400g/14oz Jerusalem artichokes, peeled

400g/14oz can white beans, drained

3½ tbsp olive oil

1 garlic clove, grated

1 tsp dried rosemary

salt and black pepper

Toppings

4 small red onions, thinly sliced

3–4 kale leaves, tough stalks removed, leaves shredded

1 handful sage leaves

3 tbsp pine nuts

2 handfuls rocket (arugula)

To make the pizza base, stir the yeast into a little of the 400ml/13½fl oz/scant 1¾ cups cold water in a large bowl. Add the rest of the ingredients and remaining water and mix to a dough. Cover the bowl with a cloth and leave to rise for at least 3 hours until doubled in size (if you're short of time you can use tepid water and leave the dough to rise for 1 hour).

Boil the Jerusalem artichokes in unsalted water until tender. Drain and blend the artichokes to a purée with the beans and olive oil. Stir the garlic and rosemary into the purée. Add salt and pepper, to taste.

Once the dough has risen, preheat the oven to 250°C/500°F/Gas 9 or the highest setting and, for the best results, place a baking stone or heavy baking tray in the oven to heat at the same time.

Divide the dough into 3–4 pieces and roll into balls. Roll out one of the balls on a floured work surface to a thin, even base. Transfer the base to a sheet of baking parchment, spread some of the Jerusalem artichoke purée over and top with the onions, kale, sage and pine nuts.

Place the pizza onto the heated pizza stone or tray in the oven and pull out the baking parchment after a couple of minutes. Bake the pizza until the base is golden, around 10 minutes. Meanwhile, roll out the next pizza base and repeat the previous step, continuing until you have used all the dough. Top the pizzas with rocket before serving.

PULLED JACKFRUIT - JERUSALEM ARTICHOKE PIZZAS

RAMEN

{serves 2}

Broth

1 brown onion, chopped

2 garlic cloves, finely chopped

4cm/1½in fresh ginger,
peeled and finely chopped

2 tbsp miso paste

1 tbsp tamari

2–4 big handfuls fresh
coriander (cilantro), leaves
and stalks separated (use
the leaves for topping)

½ chilli, deseeded

Soup

4–6 cauliflower florets, sliced

125g/4½oz/1 cup frozen
edamame (soya) beans

2 nests wheat noodles

4 mushrooms, thinly sliced

1 small leek, thinly sliced

75g/2½oz red cabbage,
finely shredded

mung bean sprouts

chilli, thinly sliced (optional)

black sesame seeds

RAMEN

I make this Japanese noodle soup all year round and simply vary the ingredients according to the changing seasons. In the winter, and around Christmas, I use cabbage, leek and frozen edamame (soya) beans or simply what I've got at home; it is a perfect way of using up vegetables and whatever is in the fridge. And it's quick too – the soup is ready in just under 10 minutes.

Blend all the ingredients for the broth (saving the coriander leaves to serve) with 500ml/17fl oz/generous 2 cups water.

Pour the broth into a pan, add the cauliflower florets and edamame and simmer for a few minutes until the edamame have softened.

Meanwhile, cook the noodles in plenty of boiling water, then drain and rinse in cold water.

Place the noodles in 2 bowls and pour over the hot broth. Top with the mushrooms, leek, red cabbage, mung bean sprouts, chilli, if using, sesame seeds and reserved coriander leaves. Serve straightaway.

📷

PAGE 151

KÅLPUDDING / CABBAGE BAKE

{serves 6}

Brown cabbage

1 small white cabbage, about 1.5kg/3lb 5oz, thinly sliced

2 tbsp rapeseed (canola) oil, plus extra for greasing

2 tbsp tamari

2 tbsp golden syrup (light golden syrup) or agave syrup

salt

Lentil mince

¼ celeriac (celery root), peeled and cut into small chunks

2 brown onions, finely chopped

5 chestnut (cremini) mushrooms, finely chopped

2 tbsp tomato purée (paste)

200g/7oz/generous 1 cup lentils (I used half green and half beluga lentils), rinsed

1 tbsp tamari

½ tsp ground allspice

2 tbsp psyllium husk

black pepper

To serve

boiled potatoes

gravy

lingonberry jam

pickled cucumber

Brown cabbage is a traditional dish on the Christmas buffet table in Skåne in southern Sweden. I have always loathed the shop-bought variety but love making my own. In fact, it was when I was about to make cabbage bake that I first tried my hand at cooking brown cabbage. Ever since then, brown cabbage has had a special place on my Christmas buffet table.

This recipe makes enough both for the buffet and for a generous pot of cabbage bake to enjoy in the days after Christmas.

〜〜〜〜〜〜〜〜

Place the cabbage in a large pan with half the oil and sauté over a medium heat until it begins to soften. Add the tamari, syrup and about 500ml/17fl oz/generous 2 cups water to cover the cabbage. Simmer over a low heat, covered with a lid, for around 1 hour until the cabbage is very tender. Add salt to taste. Pour away any remaining liquid in the pan; it's perfect to use for the gravy.

Meanwhile, make the lentil mince. In a deep frying pan (skillet), sauté the celeriac, onions and mushrooms in the remaining oil until the vegetables have softened and begin to brown. Add the tomato purée and sauté for another minute or two.

Add 500ml/17fl oz/generous 2 cups water, the lentils, tamari and allspice and simmer, covered with a lid, until the lentils are tender, about 25 minutes. The consistency of the mince should be about the same as a Bolognese sauce. Add more water if the mince is too dry. Add the psyllium husk, a little at a time, while stirring. Taste and add more seasoning, if necessary.

Preheat the oven to 200°C/400°F/Gas 6. Spoon the lentil mince into a greased ovenproof dish and top with the cabbage. Bake for 30 minutes or until the cabbage has browned nicely.

Serve the cabbage bake with potatoes, gravy, lingonberry jam and pickled cucumber.

OSTKAKA /
SWEDISH CHEESECAKE

{serves 6}

Cheesecake

1 large courgette (zucchini), peeled and cut into chunks

100g/3½oz/¾ cup blanched almonds

3 bitter almonds, grated, or ½ tsp almond extract

150ml/5fl oz/⅔ cup plant milk of your choice

140g/5oz/1 cup plain (all-purpose) flour

5 tbsp coconut or granulated sugar, or agave syrup

1½ tsp baking powder

1 pinch salt

oil, for greasing

To serve

whipped plant cream of your choice

strawberry jam

strawberries, halved

toasted chopped almonds

fresh mint leaves

For me, I cannot think about cheesecake without my thoughts turning to the big feast in Katthult, depicted in the book series 'Emil of Lönneberga', when the central character, Emil, invites the village's paupers to feast on Christmas food. This plant-based version is a little different to the original, but has the same characteristic flavour thanks to the bitter almonds.

~~~~~~~~~~~~~~~~~~~~~~~~~~~~~~~~~~~~~

Preheat the oven to 170°C/325°F/Gas 3.

Blend the courgette to a purée. Grind the blanched almonds into a flour using a nut grinder or blender.

Mix together all the ingredients for the cheesecake, including the courgette purée and ground almonds, in a bowl and pour the mixture into a greased ovenproof dish, about 25 x 18cm (10 x 7in).

Bake for 30 minutes or until the cheesecake has set and coloured a little on the surface. Leave to cool and serve topped with plant cream, jam, strawberries, almonds and mint leaves.

ICE LANTERN

Baking tins (pans) can be used for a lot more than just baking.
Here, I've used the classic bundt cake tin with a hole in the
middle to make an ice lantern. To make, fill an upturned bundt
tin with water and, if you want, add spruce sprigs or other
decorative natural materials. Place the tin outside if it's below
zero or in the freezer and leave until the water is frozen all the
way through. When frozen, the lantern can be easily removed
from the tin by rinsing it briefly under warm running water.
Place the lantern in your chosen outside spot, drop a tea light
in the hole in the middle and light when it starts to get dark.

INDEX